P.O.W.E.R.
TO GET WEALTH!

FAITH & FINANCE STRATEGY FOR THE
AFRICAN-AMERICAN COMMUNITY

JONATHAN D. MILES, M.Div., CRPC ®

Milestones Wealth & Wellness Institute, LLC
P.O. Box 7572
Atlanta, GA 30357

www.milestoneswealth.org
gotquestions@milestoneswealth.org

Ordering Information for Quantity sales:

Special discounts are available on quantity purchases by churches, corporations, associations, and others. For details, contact Milestones Wealth & Wellness Institute, LLC at the address above.

Scriptural references are taken from the King James Version of the Holy Bible unless otherwise noted.

DEDICATION

This book is dedicated to every minority person

who has struggled in their pursuit of wealth and wellness.

I come to let you know that God is about to settle the score.

I prophetically declare and decree

that God is going to grace you to do more with less

and crown you with the wisdom to strategically advance

your entrepreneurial and financial independence goals!

ACKNOWLEDGEMENTS

I am a product of my community.

This project is not about me.

This project is about those who have exemplified strength

And tenacity in the face of opposition. Through their sacrifice,

I will NEVER be broke nor suffer lack. Wealth and riches surround me!

To my Lord and savior Jesus Christ, you are the author and finisher of my faith;

Continue to perform your work within me!

To the first person who always told me that I can accomplish anything I set my mind upon,

My Mother, My Rose, Barbara Ann, I love you!

I honor her rich heritage, Samuel & Hattie Ruth Young, my maternal grandparents.

To my siblings, Lincoln, Felicia and Jasmine, you all have a special place in my heart.

To my other sister, from another mother, Ms. Stephanie Brightharp, love you!

Your love and continued support fuels my creativity.

To my Twin, Thank you Dad. Many of my characteristics are yours.

I celebrate God for the relationship that he allows us to rebuild and restore.

To my host of Aunts & Uncles I love you very much – Aunts Yvonne, Myrtis, Delores, Sarah, and Corine. The roles you all played in my life are immeasurable. To my Uncles, my strength in the shadows, I love you all very much – Uncles Sammy, Ronnie, Jearold & Carl. You always have my back and I thank you. To my paternal Grandparents – Mary Miles Chandler, Elliott "Buster" Chandler and John Miles.

To the best friends a man can have, I don't consider you my friends, you are my brothers.

Dabriun, Darrick, & Daryl.

Before I ever began to really understand who I was and the assignment I was called to do,

God called me to walk in the spirit.

Thank you to every Pastor, Elder, Intercessor and Worship Leader who has travailed with me and prayed for God's best for my life. You are warriors that I can always depend upon. Bishop QS Caldwell, Bishop Gregory Bryant & Lady Yolanda Bryant, Pastors Tony & Roz Tucker, Pastor Wanda Cail, Pastor Juandolyn Stokes, Pastor Teri Jones, Pastor Lathan Wood, Pastor Fred Ephraim, Elder Belinda Farrington, Elder Diann Jenkins, Prophet Brandon Howard, Mr. Yasin Bradley, Mr. Avery Knight, Elder John Lester and Elder Oscar Felton.

Thank you Apostle C.E. & Mother Juanita White, you birthed me in the spirit, reared me in the ways of righteousness, and gave me a foundation that will forever represent God!

Thank you Drs. Kent & Diana Branch, your leadership matured me spiritually, professionally, personally & financially. Because of you, my character matches my charisma!

Thank you Apostle Travis Jennings & Pastor Stephanie Jennings, you prove to me daily that there are higher heights & deeper depths in God that we must explore.

You continue to coach me to manifest STRONG DELIVERANCE.

You love me unconditionally. ALL THINGS ARE READY NOW!

Thank you to all of those great educators who took the time to make sure I always put my best foot forward. Mrs. Mathews (LHS), this started with you. Tell'em what you're going to tell'em, Tell'em, then Tell'em what you told them. I'm grateful! I salute all of the Men of Morehouse College and its distinguished alumnus, faculty & administration. As I sat next to many brothers that were as talented as I or even exceeded my expectations, I am forever grateful. You prepared me to embrace BLACK EXCELLENCE! To my English Literature professor who never wanted to give me an "A", but eventually I earned it in two of my last semesters, Dr. Elizabeth West, I thank you for schooling me as a scholar & a writer. You demanded my best. To the faculty, staff and administration of the Interdenominational Theological Center (ITC), I am forever indebted. It was here, that I discovered my true passion & purpose in life and understood that FAITH & FINANCE coupled with my personal pursuit for economic justice for all were the ingredients that would fuel my strategic difference.

To all of my cousins, friends & extended families that make up the Miles & Young families.

Thank you to all of my MW & W Prosperity Partners who help make this dream a reality through your prayers, donations & talents contributions to this project!

To my wife & best friend, Lena, thanks for sharing this journey with me.

I'm not perfect, but stick with me and watch God give you His best!

To every closed door of opposition, hurdles & obstacles that attempted to impede my progress,

THANK YOU. Your purpose ignited my hunger for creativity.

Now, I reclaim my time!

Contents

INTRODUCTION

---◆———○———◆---

Historically, I have seen other activists, authors and financial coaches all attempt to tackle the issue of Black Wealth in America. Honestly, the topic always seems to get off target or watered down by simple comparisons of how white Americans manage their wealth versus the various spectrums of reality that many black Americans face or deal with as we confront the issue of wealth creation in this country. When in reality, the topic of black wealth versus white wealth in this country is apples and oranges. The measuring rod from which we engage the topic is different amongst race groups. Is this fair, absolutely not! But to all of you who will read this material, whether you profess salvation or not, God's economic distribution plan for wealth and prosperity, levels the playing field! God equally distributes talents. But this world does not equally distribute opportunities. Our job is to partner with God and allow his P.O.W.E.R. to open the doors that men may not! The evidence shows that African-Americans lag behind other race groups as it relates to wealth creation that is correlated to social inequality, injustice, lack of knowledge and several other key factors that impact wealth distribution (i.e. lower pay with

1

equal amount of experience, inferiority and scare tactics in the workplace based upon racial profiling, etc.). However debt freedom, prosperity and wealth creation are not merely a matter of salvation. It's a matter of principles. If it were about salvation, then why are many of the spirit-filled believers in God's house broke and not living a maximized life in God, especially in the area of their finances? It's a matter of principles and is the reason why some of us have seen many who may not profess salvation, but still seem to live a life where they have ample means of financial resources at their disposal, and we envy the level of success their resources have afforded them. Oh, it's in the bible and it's in our churches. If it were not so, then Psalm 37 would not have addressed this issue to the church. God rains on the just (Christian believer) as well as the unjust (person who may not profess personal salvation or a relationship with God), but due to principles that fall in the space of common grace, which allows even the unbeliever to be blessed upon the principles of sowing, giving and reaping as would the Christian believer, we now understand that God truly has no respect of persons. I want every African-American, believer or non-believer, to understand that as we read this material, God has never ordained our resources to be divided based upon our indifferences or belief system, the only separating requirement, was if you participated or not (Acts 2 / Acts 5). As a mature community, we must learn to grow up with our indifferences and allow God to fill in the blanks as to how we regard one another as it relates to our personal pursuits in life. I started off as a young man in financial services almost twenty years ago and found that its environment yielded challenges to my faith and finances that fell outside of the spectrum of advice and wisdom that I was prepared to handle. So much so that it eventually landed me in career positions with built up frustration, lack of adequate pay and a looming season of spiritual, physical and financial bankruptcy! Though I struggled to put the pieces together and even seek counsel when I could, it wasn't until I really began to process the word of God in my life that was concerned about my whole man – physically, spiritually and financially- as well the instruction of a man of God who trained me well enough in giving and sowing that broke the cycle over my life. I had to practice these behaviors consistently, probably over a period of about three years, before God spoke to me in personal prayer and spoke these words, "NOW I CAN TRUST YOU!" I can remember the prophetic words that were spoken over me in the midst of the congregation, "Minister Jonathan, God said, take the people to where you are going!" If you are in the space where you struggle with consistency in your finances, there is a word for you. If you are navigating your career and still need to find ways to tweak things so that every opportunity is being maximized, there is a word for you. If you have struggled with generational bondages and hindrances in your finances and can't seem to get it together, there is a word for you! If you are well on your way, but have other loved ones who need serious help and a way of escape, there is a word for you; God has given us P.O.W.E.R. to Get Wealth! Let's go to work!

CHAPTER 1

P.O.W.E.R. to Get Wealth!

P. *O.W.E.R. to Get Wealth* *is the formula for next level living!* The backdrop of this statement is birthed from Deuteronomy 8:18. This scriptural text reflects a concern regarding "Spiritual Amnesia" for the children of Israel remembering the One giving you strength to acquire wealth. The promises of the Abrahamic covenant are linked to obedience to the laws of God. The writer reminds us that Yahweh, your God, led you through the wilderness 40 years, testing their faith and trust. During the course of this time, when they hungered, He gave them bread to eat. Similarly, the African-American community has come a long way and continues to celebrate innumerous victories that are reflective of growth and progression as a whole.

Nevertheless, our victories and triumphs still warrant observation of internal procedures to ensure that the successes of a few don't overshadow our ability to remember, reclaim and retell our stories. We must ensure that there is a passing of the baton of stewardship, to gain and maintain wealth and wellness and to strengthen communal impact so others can experience similar victories; spiritually, physically and financially. We understand that the lessons were not solely God preserving and providing for your physical necessities; there were spiritual and natural lessons to be learned as well.

P.O.W.E.R. to Get Wealth declares that the God we serve is not only concerned about our spiritual growth, but every part of our being that is impacted by the world we live in. Contrary to many of the Bible lessons we learned coming up and religious traditions that would make us think that God is only concerned about salvation and spiritual growth, we need to take time to research biblical, professional and life-application principles that will help us to excel and conquer in our pursuit to build generational wealth! P.O.W.E.R. to Get Wealth is the formula and navigation tool that will help you to accomplish the mission of setting yourself free from the financial dangers, divisions and dilemmas of your past to embrace a lifestyle of wealth and wellness that God promises to believers and all who practice godly principles of financial stewardship.

The Bible declares that man should not live by bread alone, but by every word that proceeds out of the mouth of God (Matth. 4:4). I have provided a few examples from different Bible versions to bring clarity to what God wants us to understand about the P.O.W.E.R. to Get Wealth!

Deuteronomy 8:18 declares,

KJ21

But thou shalt remember the Lord thy God; for it is He that giveth thee power to get wealth, that He may establish His covenant which He swore unto thy fathers, as it is this day.

AMP

But you shall remember [with profound respect] the Lord your God, for it is He who is giving you power to make wealth, that He may confirm His covenant which He swore (solemnly promised) to your fathers, as it is this day.

MSG

If you start thinking to yourselves, "I did all this. And all by myself. I'm rich. It's all mine!"—well, think again. Remember that God, your God, gave you the strength to produce all this wealth so as to confirm the covenant that he promised to your ancestors—as it is today.

NLT

Remember the Lord your God. He is the one who gives you power to be successful, in order to fulfill the covenant he confirmed to your ancestors with an oath.

So, He gives us strength or the ability to *get* wealth that is a component of the P.O.W.E.R. or package that is infused by the Holy

Spirit. The Bible declares that every good or generous act of giving, every perfect gift comes from above, from the Father of lights, in whom there is no inconsistency nor shadow of turning. (James 1:17). If you're reading this material, as you dig further into it and extract all of the vital resources that each chapter's lesson will provide, you will come to the understanding that prosperity has a divine cause! (Psalm 35:27) Yes, God wants to look to you to do the things in the earth that will open doors unto you, your family and your community for generations to come! Many of us have come to a place where we have been exposed to greater information, education and opportunities that allow us to experience manifestations of God's promises that were only prayed for and imagined by our ancestors. P.O.W.E.R. to Get Wealth is the fulfillment of the promise. Let's get to work!

P.O.W.E.R. is **Provision, Opportunity, Wisdom, Experience and Resilience!**

Provision (Ephesians 4:7; Assigns Grace)

Opportunity (Ecclesiastes 9:11; Affords Time)

Wisdom (Proverbs 4:7; Opens Doors)

Experience (1 Samuel 16:22-23; Brings Favor)

Resilience (Luke 18:1-8; Closes the Deal)

P.O.W.E.R. to Get Wealth is also an Apostolic expression and extension of 3 John 2, "Beloved, I wish above all things that thou mayest prosper and be in health, even as they soul prospereth!" Your P.O.W.E.R. is the ability God has given you, according to Deuteronomy 8:18, to manifest his promise unto you and your family as it relates to enlarging your territory – financially, physically and spiritually. Every class or series that I teach addresses the fact that most people who suffer in poverty or look to defeat this global epidemic, especially in minority communities, need to understand the undertaking and its undercurrent is far more extensive than the notion of financial mismanagement. Many who suffer in poverty not only have the issue of financial mismanagement, but also behavioral mismanagement! For many, these financial issues stem from a lack of resources and equal opportunities that hinder the possibility of wealth creation. For some others, their behavioral issues are directly correlated to a systemic cycle of injustice and overcompensating as a coping mechanism. In all cases, money and how we manage it, has a way of revealing who we are internally as much as the manifestation of your habits externally, both good and bad. The cycle of poverty can be broken in your family but someone has to take the responsibility to say *P.O.W.E.R. to Get Wealth* starts with me! Later on, we will discuss some of the actions you can put in place to help and share with others in your circle along your personal journey in creating transformative wealth in the lives of all God has called you to serve – FAMILY, CHURCH and COMMUNITY!

Let's explore this wealth creation formula further…..

Provision – What is in your hands? Ephesians 4:7; Matthew 25

Provision can be found in a place! God has birthed this place of provision within your hands and your heart. You have to work the provision that God has released in your life, according to your own measure (Ephesians 4:7 MSG) PURPOSE + PASSION = PROVISION; the place where God wants to provide for you exceedingly abundant above all you can ask or think.

Generally people who obtain substantial levels of wealth do it achieving or exercising natural talents, abilities or passions that are a product of their personal inclinations or general interest. Does God give us natural abilities and skillsets that are contrary to the ability we need to execute as an opportunity for provision? I generally would not think so; being able to provide substance and sustainability for our families is what drives most people daily in their profession and careers.

Opportunities – Who knows your name? (Matthew 25) Fear of rejection or getting out and proclaiming the gift & P.O.W.E.R. that God has given you to get Wealth is a thief and a robber of wealth creation! Do you know who you are.….better yet, does anyone else? What do you need to do to establish a better presence & position yourself for the promise? Mike Murdock's Wisdom Keys made me understand….we get paid for the problems we solve. If you want a presence and P.OW.E.R. that will produce the promises and prosperity of God to manifest in your life.……then SOLVE A PROBLEM! I took an assignment over fifteen years ago as it relates to retirement planning that no one wanted. As I studied the field of retirement, I began to love it and became an expert in my field. It opened doors for me, and allowed me opportunities for travel within my firm, sit on platforms within my community and began to engage product and materials to help my colleagues, family and others. **It started with an opportunity that no one else wanted!**

Wisdom – When is the best/opportune moment for me to execute my plan? This deals with getting in the game….who are your competitors….when is it time to glean vs. go forth! Count up the costs.….only a poor man takes no consideration of the decisions that lay before him and the advantages or disadvantages of each action….each can delay the promise that God has made unto you. A few years ago I made a career choice that was a bad decision.….though it was permissible and God's grace still abided with me….it was a poor professional decision that cost me five years of productive energy, money and time that is priceless! What did I feel in this situation…..how did God deal with me? Why did I make this particular decision? How do you fix or resolve the decision that has been made? Well sometimes, wisdom will tell you, what it took for you to get in the mess; you will obviously need to do the opposite to get out! Hit the rewind button! Some of us try to get out a mess we've created by pressing forward and we actually need to hit the reverse gear. Go in the complete opposite direction that you've been traveling.

Experience – How much can you give? (Romans 8:28) All things work together for good to them that love God! Both good & bad is a teacher….Who are you being influenced by? Who do you influence? Who are your mentors? (spiritual, professional, educational, etc.) what is the next move you need to take? What are the time frames involved to help you accomplish your plan?

Resilience – Why/what does it matter or mean to you? The will of the strong always survive! Ecclesiastes 9:11, "I returned, and saw under the sun, that the race is not to the swift, nor the battle to the strong, neither yet bread to the wise, nor yet riches to men of understanding, nor yet favour to men of skill; but time and chance happeneth to them all." **Persistence is the provoking of passion for the production of promise that will result in endless possibilities!**

Why give up now, break thru is on the other side! We must learn to "Weather the Financial Storms of Life"; there were seasons that were experienced in Joseph's tenure as key Strategic Advisor to

Pharaoh but his wisdom caused an entire kingdom to be sustained in the face of recession and yet experience acceleration and expansion! Storms are inevitable, but preparation is key!

Resilience involves being humble enough to go back and try AGAIN and AGAIN until it works for you! If God said it, that's enough for me! Numbers 23:19, God is not a man that he should lie, neither the son of man that he should repent, if he said it! Stand on it! Work the plan! Manifest the vision! You have P.O.W.E.R. to Get Wealth! The folly of resilience is this: sometimes pushing forward in a thing that has not manifested itself seems silly and worthless to the man who has no vision. Proverbs 13:12 (MSG) says unrelenting disappointment leaves you heartsick, but a sudden good break can turn life around! I don't know about you, but I can always use a breakthrough that takes place, SUDDENLY!

Acts 1:8 informs the Bible believer that we shall receive "power" when the Holy Spirit comes upon us and we shall be witnesses in Jerusalem (home), and in all Judea and Samaria (close proximity), and to the farthest parts of the earth (national/global). This Scripture is similar to Corinthians (1 Corinthians 12) in its explanation of Gifts of the Spirit that have different manifestation for various purposes but by the same spirit achieve what is beneficial to all! **The gifts or *P.O.W.E.R. to Get Wealth* exist for the benefit of the community as a whole, not the status of an individual**.

When God began to deal with me about the P.O.W.E.R. to Get Wealth, I heard the Holy Spirit say to me, it's the same power, but different manifestation. In the house of God, many of us have recycled myths in our families, communities and churches that wealth is a bad thing. That is a great misconception! Especially when the word of God declares that we have been given the P.O.W.E.R. to Get Wealth! So how are we are shouting, dancing and honoring our responsibilities to God and his house but going back to our brokenness, inadequacies and lack of provision in the name of God. This must not be so! I tell my students that everywhere you can trace wealth throughout the Bible it is attached to a sense of communal responsibility and an assignment to manifest wellness in the lives of others. P.O.W.E.R. according to this revelatory strategy from God as it relates to stewardship and wealth creation for kingdom-covenant givers should be intrusive, and yet have the ability to provide results through implementation and execution! When something is intrusive, it takes over and has a life of its own. Many African-Americans are now walking in the promise and manifested prayers of their ancestors who cried tears for cycles to be broken, dreams to be fulfilled and generations beyond them to be blessed! This journey is not by mere chance or circumstance. You are the change agent that will bring great release of wealth and prosperity into your family for years to come. P.O.W.E.R. to Get Wealth is a declaration that you should be making in your church and throughout your community, that you'll never be broke again!

Let's take a look in the book of Timothy,

[17] As for those who in the present age are rich, command them not to be haughty, or to set their hopes on the uncertainty of riches, but rather on God who richly provides us with everything for our enjoyment. [18] They are to do good, to be rich in good works, generous, and ready to share, [19] thus storing up for themselves the treasure of a good foundation for the future, so that they may take hold of the life that really is life.

1 Timothy 6:17-19, New Revised Standard Version (NRSV)

This passage provides an illustration that reflects the *P.O.W.E.R. to Get Wealth* but also highlights the responsibility and provisions it affords. If you think that your wealth is the result of your own hard work and efforts, then you are sadly mistaken. If you think that the wealth God has placed in your hands is ultimately for your own enjoyment and consumption, then you're even further off the path of promise for your life! This life-changing strategy for wealth creation will catapult you into a place of destiny for your family, your church, and your community. Remember, Wealth is not a coincidence. Wealth is a goal that is achieved by those who are intentional and walk in their divine purpose. The P.O.W.E.R. attributed to this life-changing formula is the combined efforts of ORGANIZED PEOPLE and ORGANIZED MONEY!

P.O.W.E.R. to Get Wealth testifies of God's promise to the believer! If God said it, put your foot on it, God will be sure to bring his Word to pass.

P.O.W.E.R. to Get Wealth provides us with the tools to understand that our seed must be targeted and intentional!

P.O.W.E.R. to Get Wealth highlights the fact that stewards will always be allowed to move to the front of the line and are gatekeepers of God's promise. Stewardship is the gateway to your becoming your own Personal Financial Manager!

P.O.W.E.R. to Get Wealth demonstrates a transition in Apostolic Authority where the borrower will become the new lender!

P.O.W.E.R. to Get Wealth authorizes a shift in the order of financial production, increase and overflow into your household! Stewards understand the demand placed upon them to prioritize needs over desires and principle over preference! This simple action of discipline has the ability to launch you into overflow!

P.O.W.E.R. TOOL #1 – Bartering (An Exchange of the Gift for the Greater)

Times have changed, at one point we had an opportunity to barter with the natural resources of the land, and although we think we have gotten away from this fad, *P.O.W.E.R. to Get Wealth* and the system of bartering reminds us of who God is and what actually takes place when we receive guidance over our finances by way of God's spirit!

What does this have to do with my prosperity? A barter system is an old method of exchange. This system has been used for centuries and long before money was invented. People exchanged services and goods for other goods and services in return. There is power in exchange! Bartering reminds us that we are not able to do everything on our own. Sometimes, you have to take your strengths, and exchange them for something greater, in order for advancement to take place!

Look at the steady transition; first goods and services, and then cash was king, now your Intellectual Property has become a medium of exchange. Intellectual Property is a work or invention that is the result of creativity, such as a manuscript or a design, to which one has rights and for which one may apply for a patent, copyright, or trademark. Knowledge and intellectual property is the new money! How you navigate this season of exchange both spiritually (hearing God for direction) and intellectually (exercising P.O.W.E.R. in your Finances) will determine the height, depth and altitude in which you are able to conquer what has the ability to change the course of your family for generations!

YOU WILL ALWAYS BE WEALTHY.......WHEN PEOPLE WANT WHAT YOU KNOW OR HAVE! – What you know or what you have does not always have to equate to CASH, but it has the P.O.W.E.R. to generate CASH!

P.O.W.E.R. TOOL #2 - Stewardship

Stewardship is a matter of maturity and the process of managing **NEEDS versus DESIRES.** What we must understand even more about stewardship is that we don't actually own anything. It is the office, duty and responsibility of managing somebody else's property, finances or household; it is also an extension of SONSHIP; YOU, own none of it, but you have **ACCESS** to ALL of it! Psalm 24:1 (TLB) states, "the earth belongs to God! Everything in all the world is his!" Our only responsibility is to allow God to move us into a position of being trusted with his assets, and in turn, he'll make provisions for our house, even the houses of our children, for generations to come!

Some of us have plagued ourselves with overthinking extenuating circumstances because we took the position of ownership of money, and in doing so, took on the responsibilities of the world that we should never have to worry about. STOP! Let's begin to practice and train ourselves now. You are just the steward and manager of God's property. If anything comes to disturb your ability to manage God's resources that have been provided to you, it should seem natural or in the best interest to consult the creator of GREAT WEALTH so as to navigate tough seasons!

Stewardship moves an individual through four (4) basic phases to accomplish God's will in the earth. The phases range from Spontaneous to Strategic as it relates to giving and saving.

Four Types of Giving/Saving: (This determines the type of seed you have in the Ground!)

1) **Spontaneous** – the person who still struggles with consistency in stewardship. They hit & miss on a consistent basis. However, with the help of God, they can become systematic in their stewardship and watch God create a path for them to flow into prosperity.

2) **Systematic** – the person who has mastered their inconsistencies but still struggle with how to maximize their potential as God's steward. This person through continuous training and practice of stewardship principles can create a competitive advantage to become one of God's foremost leaders in creating wealth & sustainability for others for generations to come!

3) **Sacrificial** – the person who has mastered systematic giving and spontaneous giving. They are ready for something different and vibrant, even something they have never experienced. Their faith moves them beyond sight to experience God's

providential care and instruction for lifestyle choices, giving and sowing into the kingdom of God. Wealth creation and sustainability is a part of their DNA, however, they must stay grounded in God for express opportunities to sow in ways that will launch them into greater!

4) **Strategic** – the person who through great consistency and application of all the prior stages of stewardship understand that targeting their stewardship for successive wealth generating opportunities is imperative for growth, even in times of recession. This person has become a coach, mentor and cultivator of change for their family, church and community for generations to come!

WHAT TYPE OF STEWARD WILL YOU BE?

Stewardship always lands you in the seat of a Financial Manager! Without inserting disciplines and principles regarding money, a strategic coach can never maximize opportunities to capitalize on time critical business endeavors. Business and money generating opportunities are always available in up or down markets, however, only those who are strategically positioned to take advantage of them typically are able to capitalize.

I'm unsure who titled the acronym P.O.O.R., meaning that poor people **Pass Over Opportunities Repeatedly!** I'm quite sure this notion of the poor person is not with intent to passively allow wealth to bypass them. It's generally hard-working people like you and I who at some point in their financial lives were just not ready to position themselves to take advantage of the opportunity – either thru lack of knowledge, money or other resources. P.O.W.E.R. to Get Wealth is the formula that levels the playing field!

Stewards and Financial Managers are concerned about **God's Leaders** and **God's House**!

Stewards and Financial Managers are concerned about their **FUTURE** and their **DESTINY**!

A Strategic Steward understands that everything from this point must be **INTENTIONAL**!

Your **SEED** as well as your **DREAMS and GOALS** should identify a **TARGET**!

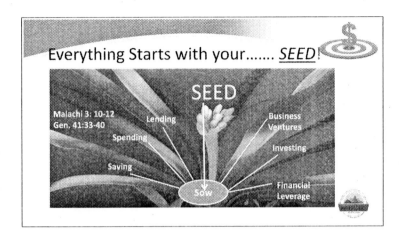

Everything Starts with your....... *SEED!*

P.O.W.E.R. TOOL #3 – Seed Sowing

So the scripture declares that God gives seed to the sower! (2 Corinthians 9:10 MSG) But what I need you to understand more emphatically is that as you sow seed, God releases P.O.W.E.R. to Get Wealth. There is an exchange in the sowing of seed that goes past your natural realm of thinking, so as to position you for greater, each according to his own measure. As you see in the illustration above, as seed is sown, it produces enough to cover savings, spending, lending, business ventures, investing and creating additional financial leverage!

We can only do (4) things with our SEED:

SOW, SAVE, SPEND and SHARE.

Every season has opportunities to sow, save, spend and share. You must discern the season you are in to identify which phase of the lifecycle quadrant you fall within. There will be times of the year when your bills are higher or at peak levels in comparison to slower times. This is a high SPENDING SEASON. These are the times that you should plan to spend more in your budget. In this case, you may find that your savings rate has been temporarily reduced; however, you can still feel confident that you are still working toward achieving milestones in wealth and wellness by reducing your debts! At this phase of the lifecycle, your sowing should remain consistent but it could mean that sharing opportunities are reduced or suspended during this time.

In times of LOW SPENDING, you may encounter opportunities to SAVE, SOW and SHARE at a greater level. Remember discernment is key and the only way we can do that with clarity and wisdom is by remaining consistent as a steward in God's house.

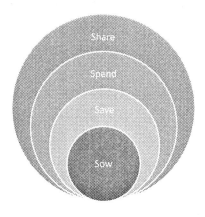

When we take care of our primary responsibility of sowing seed back into the system or ground that ultimately produces our harvest, it causes all of the other phases of the SEED Lifecycle Quadrant to SPRING FORTH!

The Law of Reciprocity says, what you make happen for God's house, God will make happen for your house! God is not the type of God that wants you to sow into his business affairs while you continue to experience lack, longsuffering and disappointments of your own. We are allowed to study the word of God and challenge God's word. It says that when we trust him according to Malachi 3, that we have a right to test him, that he will rebuke the devourer on our behalf!

You must have a TARGET identified for your SAVING…..it will ultimately dictate how you SPEND, and in that order! Using this order of importance will allow you to easily set your budget and spending habits in alignment with kingdom responsibilities and saving that are already incorporated into the plan. We're not going to even talk about sharing yet…..for all of you folks who love to give your money away to your cousins that always seem to STAY BROKE!

News flash…..THEY ARE BROKE FOR A REASON! I won't say all, but most people don't operate out of a strategic plan regarding their finances and so it's no surprise that somehow the gas or steam seems to always run out of their tanks.

Surprise……I need to borrow $1,000 dollars.

Surprise….my car is having troubles!

Surprise…..I have an emergency bill that needs to be paid.

I don't understand how it's a surprise to them; it wasn't a surprise to me! Why, because BROKE people are typical! They always run into the same issues and never have a plan. If you had a plan or savings goal in place initially, then things that will seemingly arise on occasion can be resolved out of the abundance of your **DISCIPLINED ACTION PLAN (DAP)**!

Having a 401k or workplace retirement plan (TSP, 403B, etc…) is a **DISCIPLINED ACTION PLAN.**

Having a savings account or place that you can accumulate six months of savings is a **DISCIPLINED ACTION PLAN**. There is an order to paying off debts, building an emergency fund and saving toward your retirement. You can easily accomplish maxing out your retirement savings plans just as soon as you get out of debt and build a six month savings account to account for the untimely "occasions or surprises".

Some may say, well, I don't want to just pay bills and not work toward building a savings plan or retirement account, which in turn cuts down your tax bill or reduces your taxable income at year end. Then for you, I would suggest that your investment in your retirement savings is sufficient to receive a company match (amount deposited by your employer for a minimum percentage or match deposit into your workplace retirement plan as a bonus or "sweetener" for participating in the company savings plan), which typically ranges around 3-5%. You win in this matter because you have now "paid yourself" by participating in your OWN savings plan and not relying on others to do it for you! (i.e. welfare or Social Security) However, it should be noted that anything above this amount while you may be carrying high revolving debts or low and non-existent emergency funds is self-defeating. Are you going to make over 10% returns consecutively in your workplace retirement plan funds? If not, then those retirement funds are growing at a slower rate than the debt you are compiling by carrying high interest rate credit cards that are well over 10% and growing. Take the time to assess your needs for daily living and identify what you can sow and save. These categories will dictate to you what can be spent so that it will position you well in the long term for success, growth, overflow and the ability to SHARE!

Remember I shared earlier that **everywhere you can trace wealth throughout the Bible is attached to a sense of communal responsibility for the well-being of others**. Whether it's a spouse, family, church or community, those who will have the courage to exercise their *P.O.W.E.R. to Get Wealth* will move into a greater calling to be a lender and not a borrower. Yes, I have stated that some of you are not ready to be a lender yet. God is still trying to cultivate and develop who you are and the purpose for which you were created and lending out funds and being the source for your family to resolve its issues is not your assignment YET!

I had to learn at an early age that just because I have the propensity to help and can feel the needs of others around me did not mean that I was yet ready to step into a position of providing the resources or solutions at the time. I had to grow into that place because I too was in the rat race, robbing Peter to pay Paul!

CHAPTER 2

Misconceptions about Wealth, Poverty & "The Prosperity Gospel"

———◦———

Prosperity theology (sometimes referred to as the prosperity gospel, the health and wealth gospel, or the gospel of success) is a religious belief among some Christians, who hold that financial blessing and physical well-being are always the will of God for them, and that faith, positive speech, and donations to religious causes will increase one's material wealth. Prosperity theology views the Bible as a contract between God and humans: if humans have faith in God, he will deliver security and prosperity. The doctrine emphasizes the importance of personal empowerment, proposing that it is God's will for his people to be happy.

Prosperity theology has been criticized by leaders from various Christian denominations, including within the Pentecostal and

27

Charismatic movements, who maintain that it is irresponsible, promotes idolatry, and is contrary to scripture.

In order to redefine the notion of an idolatrous theology that only positions the people to pimp God and vice versa, making God a sugar daddy that fulfills all of their wildest dreams, we must infuse the word of God to bring balance to those who argue this issue of the prosperity gospel being a crutch and a curse. The scripture declares in Matthew 4:4, that man shall not live by bread alone, but on every word that proceedeth out of the mouth of God. My Pastor and Apostle taught a lesson recently on principles versus preference. There are some things we want to do, but there are some others that we must do, to maintain our relationship and covenant with God and remain obedient to standards and guidelines that has built our faith system for generations! As we commit our ways to God's economic plan of sustainability and succession according to the word of God, we make ourselves available to him and position ourselves under an open heaven for God to pour into us spiritually, physically and financially. So it has never been just a money thing! It's always been a principles thing! Some principles are, "do unto others as you would have them do unto you." Matthew 6:33 says, "Seek ye first the kingdom of God and his righteousness, and all these things shall be added unto you." One of the foremost that stand out in my mind since I was a kid was, "give and it shall be given." The psychology of the law of reciprocity means that when someone does something nice for you, your hard-wired human nature determines that you do something nice for them in return. In other words, what you make happen in God's house, God makes it happen for you. This argument can even be suggested when we look at Haggai 1 to understand that God did not want his people to be in a place where their own homes were built up and fabulous but the house of God remained in ruins. We have an opportunity to walk in fellowship with God, understanding that relationship should be mutually beneficial! Some of us are in relationships right now that are not mutually beneficial. What do you say to these things? How does it make you feel to always be on the giving end, but never on the receiving end? However, we must also understand that in relationship; rarely do you see two parties enter into covenant offering the same incentives and strengths, yet housing the same weaknesses. There is a give and take dynamic that must be cultivated and understood by both parties and the willingness to invest at times before you see a tangible return!

So we look at our churches and we ask ourselves if there is a mutually beneficial relationship going on here that cultivates both parties involved. I would say that the answer is generally yes. However, there are times when that answer for someone will be no. Seeking God and his discernment is so crucial in times like these where we need to know the will of God in order to break generational cycles and crucify the strongman of poverty, especially in African American and other minority communities. Many of the misconceptions about wealth, prosperity and poverty are generally associated with myths that surround those who are either fortunate or less fortunate. Looks can be deceiving. What does wealth or prosperity mean to you? Is it spiritual, financial or physical? What is the measuring rod that you have determined makes this decision final in your heart, mind and in your bank account?

These are questions we need to ponder because our actions and our declarations or beliefs and values are sometimes extreme opposites and they each are speaking very loudly to your profession of wealth, prosperity and poverty, all at the same time. What are your actions and declarations saying to your children or spouse? What are your actions saying to your community? What are your actions saying in the local church where you worship?

Can we imagine for just a moment that wealth and prosperity have nothing to do with the individual, but more to do with the impact and influence to bring about change and impartation for the whole? Are there many who are wealthy and use their material wealth for selfish gain? Absolutely! However, my job is not to entertain their cause or methods of obtaining wealth. My job is to encourage the believer or even those who may not have a strong relationship with God that there are principles according to the one who gives wealth and seed to the sower that can be unlocked through the application of principles and the ability to demystify the world of finance, wealth and prosperity.

IMPACT & INFLUENCE

Are the churches of today implementing strategy to eradicate the systemic cycle of poverty or actually perpetuating frivolous

spending that is a catalyst of the widening gap and trending analysis of racial & economic inequality in America? Does the prosperity gospel message entice believers to a lifestyle of over-indulgence and consumption due to God's personal interest in our prosperity as believers?

The Prosperity Gospel's Star Player: The Miracle Seed Offering

Many of us have been partakers of the "miracle" seed pledges to our local churches only to end up realizing that seed could have been the money used to pay-down or eliminate an outstanding debt or move closer in our pursuit to obtain financial wellness. I understand that as believers, we have to walk by faith and sow into God's plan of prosperity in our lives. However, I have to address this issue because many of us give out of a spirit of pride! Your ego tells you that you have to participate in this particular time of giving, knowing that this push above your regular tithe and offering may push you right over the edge of a cliff or back into negative territory. Many times I had to eat humble pie as I sat there watching others give because my financial house was not in order. I wanted to give the sacrificial or miracle seed, but my financial status was so distraught that I had to watch others partake. I made a vow unto God, that if he would bless me to be a blessing to others, I would take care of my family, my church and my community. It is not my objective to disregard the power of the seed and the miracles it can perform, especially as we sow in faith. However,

I must share the implications that these "miracle" seeds may have in order that we walk according to knowledge (2 Peter 3:18) in our congregations.

A. Miracle Seed is not an implication that God will wipe away all of your poor spending habits just because you decided to "TIP" him today……key point, some of us want to waive a $1,000 seed in God's face as a way of condoning or signing off on our daily living of irresponsibility and frivolous spending! This should not be so.…

B. Miracle seed sowing is for the believer who has grown to a place of spiritual maturity in their giving. God cannot bless your miracle seed on top of a curse.…if you are not a systematic sower of tithe and offerings. God gives seed to the sower! (Malachi 3:8-12)

1) As my Pastor so eloquently stated, you can't go after a prophetic release of prosperity over your life but be disobedient to God at the same time.…if that's the case, you have become disqualified as your quest for wealth & riches has become UNETHICAL! Every believer is required to strive for the prize lawfully! (2 Timothy 2:5) It does not matter that your Pastor requested the "miracle" seed.…YOU know if you are a systematic sower of tithe in your local community/church and if not, that seed is NOT being sown under an open heaven! (floodgates can't be open to you, when there is a curse in place) God does not

need your money as much as he needs your obedience, obedience is better than your sacrifice!

C. Miracle seed sowing does not certify your return will come when you want, how you want! However, we trust the law of reciprocity, that whatever you do for God's house, God will make happen in your house! Sowing and reaping a harvest is a natural God ordained process. When you put seed into the ground, harvest will return….let's make sure we understand that there are no hindrances on our end through lack of knowledge that are self-defeating of our efforts.

What we must be willing to understand about seed sowing is that if you are not in a place of being a consistent tither in your local church, the windows of heaven will not be opened unto you. The first thing that should be a focus for an inconsistent tither is the matter of building consistency and trust in God's wealth distribution plan for the believer. *POWER to Get Wealth* can only be empowered through your obedience to the principles of God's Word that guide your finances, your faith and God's promise to the believer. That word informed us to *not forget* God, for in remembering him, we have a right to the inheritance that is in store for those that believe!

That's why I believe that if we first take an opportunity to build God's people, it in turn will build the church and essentially an entire community! Many believers come to church weekly with the hope that God will turn their financial situations around. I believe that this can truly take place. However, we must be mature within ourselves to know when God is pulling on us to be sacrificial, after we have mastered the level of consistency as a systematic sower of Tithe and offerings. The problem is that we rely on the Pastor's powerful message and the promise of a prophetic push (with seed in hand) to solve our misfortune, when we really should be looking for stewardship coaching and a commitment to obedience in the church. We want to put everything on our Pastor, and then come back to him or her as soon as the rent or utility bill is due and you have no money. The responsibility for this immature behavior can be on both the Pastor and the congregant. Many of these church leaders know that son or daughter can barely afford their rent and utility bills. Why not help that son or daughter become self-sufficient as opposed to using the local church as a crutch for lack of knowledge or bad behavior. If there are misfortunes, tragedy or any other obstacle that impedes the progress of the believer to sow into God's wealth distribution plan, then their stewardship coach should be able to assist and help navigate/provide guidance during that season. Every church should have a stewardship coach. This leader should exemplify, with receipts, consistent stewardship in the house of their local assembly, be in right standing with their personal obligations and their Pastors and spiritual covering, but as well be in touch with practical financial principles related to tithing, sowing, saving (401k, 403b, Investments), spending (Real Estate, Cars, Credit), and sharing (vision for your church and the community). The key point of resolution here is balance! I support seed sowing in the church that goes beyond my <u>systematic sowing</u> of tithe and offering, however the grace to shift into this next level of giving did not take place until I *mastered my consistency* in the realm of tithe and offering!

D. Why are some depending on God to bless them through sacrificial seeds but the balanced teaching of saving to workplace retirement plans and investing is not taught in our churches?

✓ I can tell you more than I want to repeat…..many times, when I interview believers from various churches that I've taught seminars, many of them state they don't consistently work at building their retirement plans and savings because most of it goes to the church. This should not be so. I have a problem when the saints, God's chosen people, are over 50 years of age and don't have $10,000 to their name, or even $5,000 for that matter. One, they are closer to retirement age and shifting their focus and spending habits should be a priority. Secondly, it does not provide equal tax benefits to gift all of your savings to local charities but negate savings to a retirement plan, which provide dollar-for-dollar reduction to taxable income and incentives. **(this is why we must teach our people how to live according to a budget and use the 70% principal – 10 save, 10 share, 10 sow policy)**

E. Wealth is not for the believer now…..I will receive my reward in heaven!

Many of you have dreams, and just like Joseph, your dreams are for an appointed time to effect change in the earth. God is looking to release stewards in the earth to accomplish greater works! The thing about stewards is that you don't own anything, but you have access to everything! The earth is the Lord's. 1 Timothy 6:17-19 says, Command those who are rich in this present world not to be arrogant nor to put their hope in wealth, which is so uncertain, but to put their hope in God, who richly provides us with everything for our enjoyment. Command them to do good, to be rich in good deeds, and to be generous and willing to share. In this way they will lay up treasure for themselves as a firm foundation for the coming age, so that they may take hold of the life that is truly life. (NIV) So why do we think God needs our money in heaven? Heaven is not bankrupt!

F. Is sacrificial seed sowing in alignment with the word of God?

Yes, when we look further in the text to even support the Kingdom principle of covenant in its relation to present day giving, sowing, tithing and sacrificial offerings, we look at various examples:

Mosaic Covenant   Abrahamic Covenant   Davidic Covenant

(sealed w/blood…)   (sealed w/circumcision…)   (2 Sam 7 – sealed w/eternal praise)

The common thread of all covenant established between God & his people was that it was <u>sealed</u>, <u>empowered,</u> <u>watered</u> or <u>validated</u> by SACRIFICE. Whether we move from Old Testament or New Testament teachings, the Bible teaches us that obedience and commitment to God's agenda as opposed to our own has always been rewarded and tested through man's sacrifice. For those who even dispute tithe and offering as an Old Testament requirement and no longer relevant, even with Jesus' sacrifice on the cross, God ordained sacrifice as an assurance that will always undergird the believer's push toward advancing the purposes of God in the kingdom. No longer do we sacrifice the items of Old Testament – bullocks, sheep and oxen. We commit our time, talent, tithe and treasure unto God.

G. Why must we build people from the order of basic to advanced techniques in sowing seed in the kingdom?

✓ Sowing seed in the kingdom of God has never been out of order. However, many times the motivation of the sower gets out of alignment. Tithe and offerings are foundational Christian principles used to build your faith and trust in God's plan to advance his purpose through you for his kingdom.

✓ Sowing seed outside of normal tithe and offering is an advanced kingdom finance tool that should only be exercised by mature believers who are already committed to the systematic commitment of tithe and offerings in the house of the Lord. Miracle seeds and pledges typically only come to those who have implemented plans to track their spending habits and strategically seek to advance the kingdom of God, even in spontaneous times. (2 Corinthians 9:10)

Myths & Misconceptions surrounding the Wealthy

As I committed myself to researching and providing information that would be vital to implementing healthy habits within the African-American community for transformative wealth practice, I found an online article on The Motley Fool that made references to several myths regarding the wealthy that are perpetuated in our society. Many of them reveal that most people's story to building wealth are not cookie-cutter experiences that have to be the same for everyone, nor do they resemble the spoiled rich kid whose lust for greed and power become reality simply because of the silver spoon he or she has been fed since infancy. Many people have different stories. Bottom line, do the work, seek God and professionals for help, and write your own narrative!

Myth #1: Wealth Creation Depends on Your Level of Education

The greatest teacher is life itself. It presents problems and stumbling blocks that must be overcome. There would be no millionaires who achieved wealth on an inadequate education if that were so. Today's education system shows you how to get a job; it does not show you how to become financially wealthy. It does not teach you how to get along with others for mutual profit. Many people work hard for 40 years but have little to show at retirement. The wealthy have financial and time freedom simply because they learned the methods to get that way through a great deal of trial and failure. It's calculated that only 2% have the knowledge to acquire wealth and be successful and little of that comes from a college education. Many people have risen from poverty to become multi-millionaires and did so without any formal education. While education is important, a BA or PhD does not guarantee great wealth. Many who were born into wealthy families became destitute and died penniless. Education can point you in the direction that leads to wealth, but it cannot take you by the hand and lead you there. So the better question is, what type of education have you developed relative to the field or place of provision that God has called you to prosper? The correlation of education to success depends upon your using these tools to remain relevant and forward-thinking in your field of expertise!

Myth #2: You Must Exchange Time for Money

If you earn a salary you are indeed trading time for money. But it is not completely true. Investments, residual income, capital gains and inheritances are ways that provide money without it being earned. Affiliate opportunities abound on the Internet that can bring an income well above the effort and time spent. Many earn substantial money by selling information without building a website or doing anything more beyond advertising their business. It's production that creates income, not the time taken to create it.

Myth #3: Working Hard Will Make You Rich

This is the age old advice passed down from generation to generation. Many people work hard throughout life, yet never become wealthy. Working hard is a good trait to have, but it does not guarantee wealth. Hard work has to be leveraged so the best use of time and energy produces more money. In fact working hard has a negative impact on health. High stress and worry lead to high blood pressure and heart disease. Those who succeed work hard simply for the enjoyment and not because they must pay their bills.

Myth #4: To Succeed, You Need to Improve Your Weaknesses

That's holds true for any character flaws that prevent you from associating with those people who can help you succeed. Too many people are selfish and don't understand that success is based on how much they help others. But you can never be perfect. You have certain strengths and weaknesses. You cannot be skilled in everything, nor would you wish to. Businessmen are not lawyers, bankers and accountants. It would be a waste of time to improve on those areas that don't compliment your skills.

Myth #5: Stay Away from Risk

Life is full of risk. Decisions can go bad. Playing safe with the way you do things does nothing to challenge creativity and problem solving. You take risks when you choose a career in a field that could become obsolete tomorrow. You take risks that the woman or man you marry may decide to abandon the relationship. Taking risks is the only way to learn anything through life. Playing safe leads to stagnation. On the other hand, there are times when playing safe is the best course of action. You do need to get as much information before you take risks. Successful people know when to take a risk and when to leave it alone.

Myth #6: They live in huge houses and drive expensive cars

Having all of the latest and greatest perks from technology to housing, driving, clothing and plenty of cash to spend frivolously is not an interest of most wealthy individuals. One of my favorite readings of the past, *The Millionaire Next Door*, found in studies of the wealthy that most households with a net worth over $1 million lived in middle-class neighborhoods and eschewed status purchases. Looks can be deceiving! Many get away with trying to look wealthy, but their financial statements tell an extremely different story! That's why I stress, 'faking it 'till you make it' is the motto of yesterday!

Myth #7: Rich people are happier because they are rich

There's a mountain of research showing that increases in income only boost happiness levels up to a certain point. Once you have enough expendable income that you can cover your needs and do the things you generally enjoy without worrying about your finances, adding more money to the mix doesn't upgrade your emotional well-being. So why are the rich happier? It's often because they either have experienced a good deal of success in their fields, or because they have greater freedom of time. Remember, sometimes you have to do what you have to do, so you can do what you want to do! The rich just get to that point earlier than most.

Myth #8: A wealthy lineage explains why the rich are rich

According to Wealth-X, here's how the world's 2,170 billionaires came by their fortunes:

60% were entirely self-made

20% were a combination of self-made and inheritance

20% were purely a result of inheritance

No one is arguing that coming from a wealthy family doesn't help. However, the reality shows that 60-80% of most people will not acquire wealth through the result of inheritance. What is your plan to become financially independent as you develop the purposes and passions that God has placed on the inside of you?

Myth #9: Rich people never go bankrupt

Sell this story to many of the athletes and professional entertainers who have acquired great wealth during their careers, only to lose it to bad investments, poor spending habits or lack of involvement in their own financial matters that turned disastrous over time. However, there's a hard and fast truth that no rich person can get around: if you spend more that you bring in, you'll eventually go bankrupt Young people see success as looking, feeling and acting like fashion models, sports heroes and music stars. They strive to match the image of the herd, to blend in. Real success starts from developing your own unique talents and building the right team to help cultivate that wealth.

Myths & Misconceptions surrounding Poverty

Myths about poverty in the world's wealthiest nation

Myths and misunderstandings fuel stereotypes that negatively impact those living in poverty in the U.S. Here are just a few of many related to U.S. poverty:

Myth: Even if you're poor in the U.S. you're doing pretty well.

The Reality: The U.S. ranks near the bottom of the world's wealthiest countries in how well it cares for its children in poverty. Out of 24 nations, the U.S. ranked between 19th and 23rd in critical areas of health, education, and material well-being. *(UNICEF, 2010)*

Myth: No one goes hungry in America.

The Reality: One in six Americans lives in a household that is "food insecure," meaning that in any given month, they will be out of money, out of food, and forced to miss meals or seek assistance to feed themselves. Nationally, more than 50 million Americans were food insecure in 2011—a 39 percent increase from 2007. Among the hungry are nearly 17 million children. *(U.S. Dept. of Agriculture, 2012)*

Myth: Poverty has little lasting impact on children.

The Reality: Research is clear that poverty is the single greatest threat to children's well-being. Poverty can impede children's ability to learn and contribute to social, emotional, and behavioral problems. Poverty also can contribute to poor physical and mental health. Risks are greatest for children who experience poverty when they are young and/or experience deep and persistent poverty. *(National Center for Children in Poverty, 2012)*

Myth: Few U.S. children are homeless

The Reality: More than 1.6 million of the nation's children go to sleep without a home each year. Homeless children experience a lack of safety, comfort, privacy, reassuring routines, adequate health care, uninterrupted schooling, sustaining relationships, and a sense of community. These factors combine to create a life-altering experience that inflicts profound and lasting scars. *(National Center on Family Homelessness, 2012)*

Myth: All U.S. children have equal opportunities to succeed in school.

The Reality:

- Children born poor, at low birth weight, without health coverage, and who start school not ready to learn often fall behind and drop out.

- **Teachers in high poverty schools are more likely to have less experience, less training, and fewer advanced degrees than teachers in low poverty schools**.

- 22 percent of children who have lived in poverty do not graduate from high school, compared with six percent of those who have never been poor.

- 32 percent of students who spent more than half of their childhoods in poverty do not graduate.

(Children's Defense Fund, 2010; Annie E. Casey Foundation, 2012)

Myth: People who are poor are lazy.

Fact: More than 10.5 million people in poverty formed the "working poor" in the U.S. in 2010, meaning they were in the labor force for at least 27 weeks. *(U.S. Department of Labor, Bureau of Labor Statistics, 2012)*

Myth: Those living in poverty just want to stay there.

Fact: Millions of Americans move in and out of poverty over a lifetime. More than half the U.S. population will live in poverty at some point before age 65. *(Urban Institute, 2010)*

Studies regarding poverty on www.worldvisionusprograms.org, retrieved on Jan. 13th, 2018

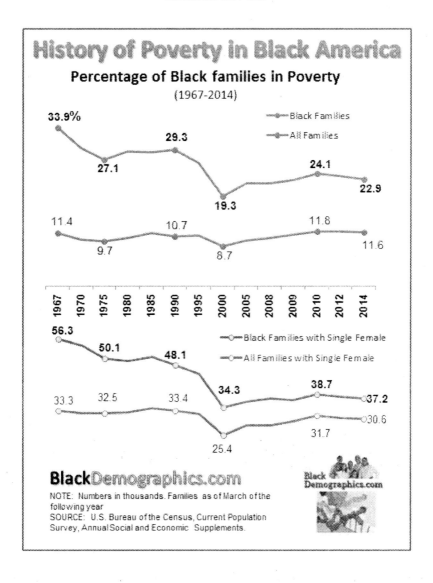

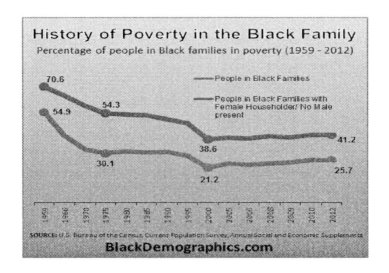

As you reflect over the images that have been provided above, did you know that over 40% of African-American households are led by single women? This is an alarming number for African-Americans because much of the systemic poverty that exists for Black America stem from this marginalized group and her children! So as the cultivator of communication and change for those who stand behind us looking for an answer, we must ask the following questions:

What efforts can be incorporated to minimalize the impact of this growing epidemic?

- Support groups
- After-care programs
- Employment assistance or training (promote higher wages)
- Accountability efforts for Fathers
- Co-parenting programs

- Community involvement & Family First Facilities

- Financial Literacy Training & Education

As it relates to all other African-American households that fall outside of the category of single-parenting by mothers, over 33% of African American households vs. the General population support children and grand-children under the age of 18. The inequality of single black mothers and the African-American family in general, impact our legacy- the involvement, supervision, aspirations and mobility of their children. This is our community! The history of poverty in the black family hinders constructing healthy families and communities. While the prosperity gospel may have caused some of the systemic financial challenges in our churches along with congregants that sunk their belief and money into it, the Bible gives us great examples of a systematic process on how to achieve and maintain economic sustainability; especially in times of lack. Misconceptions and a false perception of what really takes place in our families, our churches and our communities across the United States coupled with racial bias and discrimination that hinder the progression of a people is what fuels and perpetuates much of the socio-economic inequality and widening wealth gap amongst race groups.

CHAPTER 3

From the Pit to the Palace

———◆—❍—◆———

God is raising up the spirit of Joseph within you to lead your family, your community, and your church to influence the world. I decree and declare that God is raising up a generation of global movers and shakers for the kingdom, who will adhere to the voice of God in their business dealings and financial matters to influence the world! Every disappointment that you've endured was only a stepping stone to focus your energies in the right place for such a time as this! You were not born to prosper everywhere. Your destiny, determination and differentiation will flourish in the place that God has assigned unto you for kingdom purpose. Just like Joseph, our thinking has to be gradually transitioned as we are exposed to greater wealth. Joseph's dreams became more apparent to him at the young age of seventeen, while he was already at work in his father's field. Those dreams did not manifest until he was thirty years old and chief administrator over Pharaoh's kingdom. Dreamers, be still and know that God is on your side! Any dream that has the ability to blow your mind needs time to be cultivated. As kingdom financiers who are prophetically declaring and walking in the *P.O.W.E.R. to Get Wealth*, your financial awareness and knowledge has to be equivalent to the level of responsibility that is NOW in your possession!

Now that doesn't mean that we will all become financial experts overnight, nor does it obligate us to take financial courses equivalent to those financial professionals who instruct us in areas of our lives. However, we must be aware, ask questions, and have a working knowledge of the promises that God has bestowed upon us so that we are aware of Satan's devices and attacks that hinder our finances and allow our lack of knowledge to hold us hostage to financial bondage, curses and generational poverty!

This biblical narrative of Joseph takes shape in the 37th chapter of Genesis. My purpose of this illustration is not for you to become a biblical scholar, that's what the preacher is for, but I would like to highlight key components of his transition into P.O.W.E.R. that catapulted his career into Great Wealth and influence throughout all of Egypt and Israel. God always gives spiritual keys that have a master-code to unlock all of the treasures of this world. The Word of God lets us know in Proverbs 13:22 that the wealth of the wicked is laid up for the righteous!

JOSEPH'S CAREER PATH:

DREAMER (yet, full of youthful pride & arrogance)

THROWN INTO A PIT

SOLD INTO SLAVERY

SENT TO PRISON

SERVING IN THE PALACE

Joseph's career path and transitioning into P.O.W.E.R. to Get Wealth began in a Pit. Many of us who may be unfamiliar with this story should also note that this transition from the Pit to the Palace extended over 13 years! Genesis 37 tells us that Joseph was a young man, seventeen years old, as his testimony of perseverance began to unfold. He endured the hatred and jealousy of his brothers who knew that he was favored by their father. It wasn't until age thirty, that Joseph realized the manifestation of dreams that he experienced in his younger years as he took his rightful place as chief caretaker and advisor to Pharaoh in the palace. We must understand what we were created to do and also understand that the gifts and grace that requires sharpening does not always present itself in its early stages.

This transition of power, prosperity and purpose is a testament to those who have been discouraged in their journey of P.O.W.E.R. to Get Wealth; that all is not lost. The pit was symbolic of rejection, conformity, emptiness, exile and lack of life and vitality. Sounds familiar? We too have been born with dreams, visions and various talents according to our measure that God has bestowed upon us to manifest wealth, health and spiritual destiny in our personal lives and the lives of those we impact. **Many of us get sucked into a dead space where others who don't believe in your vision or aren't mature enough to help cultivate it and respond by throwing you and your dream into a pit!** They try to conform it, reject it, exile it, revamp it; so that it becomes something else all-together. The dream is now positioned outside of the will of God and His ability to bless it and cause you to prosper. But when God has a plan to prosper and promote you, there's nothing in this earth that can stop God's love from finding you where you are and transitioning you from the Pit to the Palace!

However, even as we know there are transitions you make when dealing with your profession and your money, you too must transition mentally and emotionally to produce P.O.W.E.R. to Get Wealth!

There are three (3) things you will encounter in your profession & in your money when attempting to transition from the Pit to the Palace, while pursuing a lifestyle of wealth and wellness and positioning yourself for P.OW.E.R. to Get Wealth:

A. Character Assassination (Gen. 37)

B. Character Accusation (Gen. 39)

C. Character Affirmation (Gen. 41)

Character Assassination

Character assassination starts, before you get started! Its goal is to attempt to make sure this wagon never leaves the barn. Doubt, misunderstanding, rejection, conformity and obstruction are examples of this stage of transitioning from the Pit to the Palace and pursuing P.O.W.E.R. to Get Wealth! Just like Joseph's brothers, everyone will not receive the assignment of P.O.W.E.R. to Get Wealth, because they are not the strategic planners and strategists that will catapult their family, their church and their community into its rightful place of destiny. Everyone is not capable of carrying that mantle. So the non-believer will kill you, before he or she cultivates you! They just don't understand that their jealousy or lack of revealed knowledge clouds their understanding. Your personal promotion is key to the success of your family, your church and the community as they journey into financial independence.

Character Accusations

Congratulations! You've been promoted to your next level of haters that can't understand your wanting to move past the place of poverty, lack, and scarcity, into the place that God has promised he would prosper you as an act of your will to remember him in your journey. Since the first level didn't kill you, the second level only comes to distract you from the FOCUS, FAVOR and the FORTITUDE needed to continue the journey until manifestation takes place. Level Two (2) comes with new tactics, principalities and powers to stop us from aggressively pursuing the very thing that God ordained to bless you for a lifetime! On this level, LIES are told. ACCUSATIONS are made. Anything to distort God's truth in your life is the mission of this level so that its smokescreen causes you to be sidetracked and abort the mission and agenda God purposed for you to fulfill! Before you enter into your greatest level of responsibility that God has commissioned, your level of integrity will also be tried. In the 39th chapter of Genesis, Joseph had to endure accusations from a formidable opponent, Potiphar's wife. She was a woman of influence and prestige, since she was the wife of the man 2nd in command to Pharaoh. Her voice had reach and impact. So much so that it landed Joseph in jail as she accused him of sexual assault. Even false accusations have a window of opportunity to distort, damage and even defame your character. However, false accusations are just that. Once its shelf-life has come to a close, truth has to take over and outshine the residue of the smokescreen. In a season of character accusations, one has to remain focused on the goal at hand and strategically pursue God's purpose and promise for their lives without regret.

Character Affirmation

You've stood the test of time. And just like Joseph, you have gone through life's obstacles. However, even the enemy of your progression didn't see that God has a purpose for your life's plan, he prepared you for life's obstacles and he's already making provision for life's rewards. You too have been in a low place in your career and in your finances. I prophesy today, that God is about to take you from your low place, into the HIGH PLACE! God is about to transition you from pit thinking to PALACE planning! The place where your accusers left you, Joseph, is the place where God is meeting you to set you up for a lifetime of TRIUMPHANT REIGN!! The objective of this level will transition your mind and your money into MILESTONES of wealth and wellness! The 41st chapter of Genesis allows us to understand that in spite of all, Joseph endured sabotage and shame from those even closest to him that rejected his dreams, cast his dreams into a pit, sold him into slavery, and slandered his name with accusations. Nevertheless, Joseph never stopped dreaming. You are destined to walk into the greatest season in your life, if you dare to believe the plan God has in store for you! **The same gift that was the cause of his arrogance, self-righteousness and presumptuous behavior as a young man, is the same gift that served and catapulted him to a place of high-ranking authority and wisdom as a mature man in Pharaoh's Palace.** For those brave enough to weather the storms of assassination and accusation en route to a life filled with promise and affirmation, you must accept that God is the greatest power and we shall not be defeated! Just like Joseph, we will begin to make transitions in our strategic alignments and our associations. God always prepares kingdom financiers for high-level strategic thinking, planning and problem-solving. Joseph's ability to solve Pharaoh's problem, was his ticket to forming a strategic alliance with the one who would catapult his future and everything attached to him (family, community, etc)!

As mentioned in Chapter 1, in order to shift from SPONTANEOUS/SYSTEMATIC TO SACRIFICIAL/STRATEGIC, God must be able to trust you to **CULTIVATE** and not **CONSUME.**

JOSEPH'S CAREER PATH:
DREAMER (yet, full of youthful pride & arrogance)

THREW INTO A PIT

SOLD INTO SLAVERY

SENT TO PRISON

SERVING IN THE PALACE

In one 14-year period, because of careful and diligent savings during seven prosperous years, Joseph was able to buy everything that could be bought in the land of Egypt over the next several years of economic recession.

Joseph Principle's Theme:

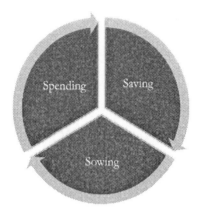

Every economic season/cycle…..can be conquered thru <u>Discipline</u> & <u>Discernment</u>.

A seasoned Steward must know how to manage all aspects in each season that is encountered!

<u>Save & Sow in prosperous times</u> (ECONOMIC EXPANSION/GROWTH) when others are spending frivolously

<u>Spend & Share at reduced prices</u> (ECONOMIC RECESSIONS) when others are desperate to sell because they need liquidity and resources. (Think about annual gifting….clients are inclined to gift out of lower cost basis due to the fact that gains in their portfolio will be written off by the gift. If they sell those with higher cost basis to realize left over gains....they can now have lower tax implications when it's time to pay Uncle Sam)

Thus, the Joseph Principle is built on (3) key truths:

1) There are cycles of prosperity and recession in every economy.

2) During times of prosperity, surpluses should be saved and invested, not consumed!

3) In times of recession, that surplus can be multiplied into more wealth as it is used to help meet the needs of others.

Economic Cycles are inevitable, though hopefully not as severe as the two seven-year cycles that Joseph saw in his lifetime. Just as there is a time to plant and a time harvest, there is a time to put more into our storehouses and a time where we may need to put in less. There will also be a time to give out of our storehouses and a time to replenish them, or we may do a combination of both. There is also a time to invest our savings conservatively, and a time God may instruct us to use it to build wealth more aggressively. Just as Solomon said in Ecclesiastes:

(Ecclesiastes 3:1-3)

For everything there is a season,

a time for every activity under heaven.

[2] A time to be born and a time to die.

A time to plant and a time to harvest.

[3] A time to kill and a time to heal.

A time to tear down and a time to build up.

(Matthew 5:45; 7:24-27)

Matthew 7:24-27 The Message (MSG)

[24-25] "These words I speak to you are not incidental additions to your life, homeowner improvements to your standard of living. They are foundational words, words to build a life on. If you work these words into your life, you are like a smart carpenter who built his house on solid rock. Rain poured down, the river flooded, a tornado hit—but nothing moved that house. It was fixed to the rock.

[26-27] "But if you just use my words in Bible studies and don't work them into your life, you are like a stupid carpenter who built his house on the sandy beach. When a storm rolled in and the waves came up, it collapsed like a house of cards."

In other words, cycles of nature and circumstances don't only happen to bad people, they happen to everyone. Those who are wisely prepared for them are the ones who "weather" the storms. Those who build their houses – in the financial realm as well as in the other areas of our lives – live firmly on the Word of God and His principles, will

60

not only survive these storms but will often be stronger afterward. Joseph's transition required his understanding of the following concepts:

✓ **The Greater Your Wealth, the Greater Your Levels of Responsibility!**

A. As Joseph was assigned greater levels of responsibility, he leaned on the Lord for instructions and directives for all of his family, Pharaoh's house and all of Egypt! Wealth should not draw us away from God, but draw us closer to God! What does God want us to do with our access? What influential moves need to be made? What is the plan for your family? What is the plan for your church? What is the plan for your community?

B. In order to shift from SPONTANEOUS TO STRATEGIC, God must be able to trust you to **CULTIVATE** and not **CONSUME.** Shifting from Spontaneous (Immature Giver) to Strategic (Mature/Kingdom Financier), one must expect even as Joseph did, that the transition will come with several bumps along the road to growth

C. Other Bible Figures who had the responsibility to Build God's House & His People include Nehemiah, Haggai, etc…there's a blueprint to building a dynasty & inheritance that will last generations….are you up for the task?

✓ **Great Wealth gives birth to Great Access!**

Many of our black athletes, artists & performers that transition into great wealth almost overnight get caught up in a system where they are now expected to understand that they can't initially pay all of their families bills, have an entourage (where no one has real careers or passions of their own) and carry an entire city on their shoulders. They are still unprepared to be responsible with the new access that they have been granted. Because the basics are not in place (budgeting, disciplined savings/action plans, tax & estate planning, etc.) they begin to outsource everything they aren't familiar with only to find out they may not have made the best choices or chosen the best people to serve in various capacities! It ultimately BANKRUPTS them, emotionally, spiritually and financially! Access is everything. If you are not ready for open doors, it has the potential to paralyze your purpose and progression!

✓ **Great Wealth requires a Great Mind!** (To manage growth & sustainability) we cannot put new wine in old wineskins! New wealth requires new ideas! Simply banking your money and traditional savings accounts are the thoughts of yesterday....what types of investments are available to you in this new financial arena? Real estate? Investment portfolios? Private investment opportunities? The earth is the Lord's and the fullness thereof.....you may not know how to manage large assets, but God does! Trust the source from which great wealth

flows from!

CHAPTER 4

War Until You Win

———————◆———○———◆———————

Poverty is a SPIRIT! And just like any other devil….God is able to deliver you from your strong enemy! Death and life are in the power of the TONGUE! (Prov. 18:21) You will never conquer what you're unwilling to confront! Many minority communities still unknowingly battle a pervasive systematic cycle of low self-esteem and underachieving goals as a by-product of chattel slavery. It's only until you free your mind, will you be able to navigate the cycle of poverty and brokenness that exists within your family or community that will open the door and cause you to win! Poverty is a mindset that must be administered to as if it's a global epidemic or clinical disease. Poverty has the ability to destroy the potential of your purpose and your potential for promise! Poverty has the ability to change the outcome of a man, his family and his community. On the other hand, stewardship, the actual management of God's property, is an essential component of worship and true showmanship of God's ability to trust those in covenant with him regarding seed and the sower, a key element to achieving a prosperous lifestyle of wealth and wellness. We know that 2 Corinthians 9:10 says, Now He who provides seed for the sower and bread for food will provide and multiply your seed for sowing [that is, your resources] and increase the harvest of your righteousness [which shows itself in active goodness, kindness, and love] (AMP). However, we must also understand that we have an enemy whose primary purpose is to get us to disengage from this covenant agreement with God that will ultimately result in us living a lifestyle of poverty, lack and not enough. Subsequently, a lack of resources minimalizes our acts of righteousness and service unto God causing our efforts to go dormant and without the progression that is needed to advance a community. Whether we are committed to the cause or not, if you are reading this material and your finances are not in the place you feel they should be, or if you seem to always struggle in the pursuit of financial independence and freedom or even if you make great money but the resources you have and the impact money has in your life and in the lives of those you influence don't add up, then I must suggest to you, the enemy has you in a headlock, and you've been oblivious to the attacks of Satan!

The Kingdom of Heaven suffers violence, but now it's time for you to take your prosperity back, by force!

5 Things you need to know to War against the Spirit of Poverty....Until you Win:

1) **Prayer Unlocks** the Plans to Strategic Victory

2) **Praise Unfolds** the Key to Strategic Victory

3) **Purpose & Passion Unveils** the Secrets/Strategy of the Wealthy

4) **Practice Undergirds** the P.O.W.E.R. of Strategic Transformation

5) **Performance Upholds** P.O.W.E.R. to Get Wealth and turns Strategic Victory into Legacy

Proverbs 6:10-11 MSG says,

[6-11] You lazy fool, look at an ant.

Watch it closely; let it teach you a thing or two.

Nobody has to tell it what to do.

All summer it stores up food;

at harvest it stockpiles provisions.

So how long are you going to laze around doing nothing?

How long before you get out of bed?

A nap here, a nap there, a day off here, a day off there,

sit back, take it easy—do you know what comes next?

Just this: You can look forward to a dirt-poor life,

poverty your permanent houseguest!

Poverty has a history in this country that has been intrusive and unrelenting in its attack on the African-American family. This war has been told for a long time and evidenced through statistical data that tracks the history of our unfolding as a community and the aftermath of enslaved bodies and minds that are the catalyst for poverty and further implosion that begins with fatherlessness, single-parenting, and cycles of bad behavior. THIS CYCLE MUST BE BROKEN!

During the early years of my career, I had to battle a roller coaster of emotions and financial instability due to lack of preparation (knowledge) and low wage earning opportunities. No wonder most of us have difficult and emotional baggage when dealing with out of control spending habits. Although many have come along to attempt to nullify its profound impact on an entire race, numerous geographic areas across the United States that were most prevalent in slave trade and the many years of systemic racial injustices battle with systemic over-indulgence and coping behaviors that highlight feelings of frustration and pent up resentment of poverty and its impact on our families. This writing material is not an attempt to incite any feelings of our history for the sake of violence or retribution by way of inappropriate behavioral conduct, however, we must acknowledge the pain of our history so we can finally move forward as a community and create new positive change for legacy and sustainability. How must

African-Americans begin to engage the conversation of financial literacy in an environment that embodies safe-space where we can share our concerns, motivations or inadequacies without judgment? What does it mean to "War until I Win"? The Biblical illustration found in Ephesians 6, is not just a battle for spiritual fervor and positioning, it also includes the war that has been waged against minority communities that are not just against people or principalities, but systems. (the rulers of the darkness of this world – spiritual wickedness in high places)

According to the **2014** U.S. Census Bureau ACS study (see charts below) **27% of all African American men, women and children live below the poverty level** compared to just 11% of all Americans. An even higher percentage **(38%) of Black children live in poverty** compared to 22% of all children in America. The poverty rate for **working-age Black women (26%)** which consists of women ages 18 to 64 is higher than that of **working-age Black men (21%)**.

Poverty rates for Black families vary based on the family type. While **23% of all Black families live below** the poverty level **only 8% of Black married couple families live in poverty** which is considerably lower than the **37% of Black families headed by single women** who live below the poverty line. The highest poverty rates **(46%)** are for Black families **with children** which are headed by **single Black women**. This is significant considering more than half **(55%) of all Black families with children are headed by single women.**

So when we talk about warfare and its strategic findings, we must understand that financial stability and rather independence is a major undertaking for these groups that have been marginalized through death, divorce, desertion or demographic profiling. We wrestle not against flesh and blood, but against principalities, powers and the rulers of this world to strategically support sustainability efforts of this group and the children and community it impacts. I understand, we all do not fall into this category. However, we all have a mother, sister, friend, relative or someone we know that may fall into this war against poverty. It's simple. Together we win, divided we fall!

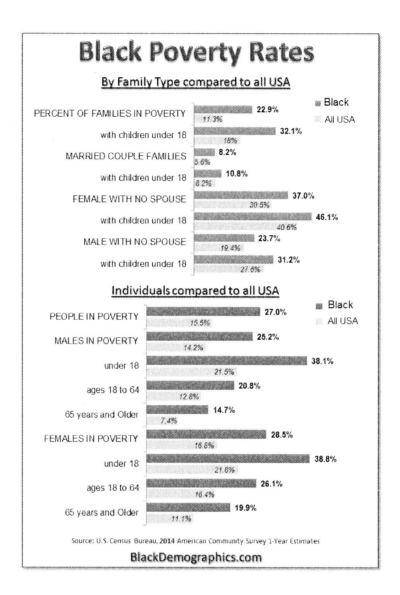

"Warring until you Win", involves a multi-step process or methodology for success. It involves theory, application and demonstration.

Prayer – Unlocking the Plan to Strategic Victory; We must pray until we have Purpose, Passion and a PLAN!

One of my favorite bible stories comes from Joshua 7, the story of Achan. This biblical illustration shows us that there are times when the presence of God is strong and evident, and then there may be times when it is not. Well, in this biblical narrative, the writer unfolds the story that the children of Israel had just come out of battle and conquered their enemy at the wall of Jericho. Surely God was with them! However, God gave the children of Israel a directive as it concerned Jericho and her spoils. Rahab and her family were the only inhabitants to be spared along with all the silver, gold and vessels of brass and iron that were to be consecrated unto the Lord. Achan, one of the sons of the tribe of Judah, had taken amongst the spoils, Babylonian garments, silver and gold for himself. This act of disobedience by Achan had a devastating impact on an entire group of people. Joshua sought the Lord in prayer with determination for direction. His diligence in prayer ultimately provided instructions that would identify the cause, the curse and the culprit! It was in this instance I learned several key principles that are relative even to financial stewardship:

A. Prayer has the ability to identify your enemy & provide instructions to annihilate their plans

B. Stealing is an offense of epic proportion in the sight of God

C. Anytime you don't obey God's commands, you make yourself vulnerable to attacks

D. God doesn't bring you out of a storm, to throw you right back in…(unless the lesson has not been learned)

E. You can't stand before your enemy while under a curse

F. God can't fight for you, until the curse is removed

G. Where there's a curse, there's always a culprit!

For many of us, our enemy is poverty. It has wreaked havoc in our families for generations and it's time for the bleeding to stop! We think God is impressed that we do "whatever is necessary" to feed our families. It essentially dismisses his Lordship. We think because the Lord has been on our side in the past, surely he'll be there in the future. That assumption dismisses the fact that he's still a God of judgment. We think because we tipped God last week that he's impressed. God still hastens to perform his word. A curse is a curse. Many of us think that our enemy is a person, place or thing. Many times the enemy of your soul, purpose and passion comes from a familiar place and we must be diligent about identifying the root cause of poverty or lack of progression that may exist in our families! When we are faithful, as Joshua was in this text, the spirit of the Lord will take you directly to your enemy. God will reveal to you the curse and the culprit! Many of us are fighting generational poverty, generational depression, generational lack of knowledge and a host of other generational associations that hinder our flow of prosperity and management of God's resources to bless our family, community and our church. We must target these enemies in prayer and allow God to give us effective warfare and exit strategies! Your personal prayer time should not only be communication unto God but also an opportunity for a spiritual download that releases strategy for effective implementation. Who is the enemy that targets your finances? Why are you being targeted? How do you enter a place of retreat and recovery until seasons change?

Praise Unfolds the Key to Strategic Victory

A worshipper should never go into the presence of God & come out empty-handed! I say this with full conviction and experience to back it up. One of the most passionate and intimate pursuits in God is the ability to worship. Worship allows us to encounter the very presence of God, where there is fullness of joy and in his right hand, pleasures forevermore. That being said, I had an experience years ago that taught me a lot about personal worship and its strength. I was a worship leader for many years, dedicated to the things of God and entrusted with the assignment to lead others into the presence of God on a weekly, recurring basis. I was younger then and didn't understand that the very God I excelled in worship with was the same God who also cared about my personal life and my ability to live a quality life; spiritually, naturally, physically and financially. Many times I questioned my level of sacrifice to the things of God because it seemed that my ability to live a quality life were not manifesting -- even just having the necessities of life – food, shelter, and clothing. I first had to address my own level of inconsistency, and then I turned to address the reason why a quality life in God avoided me personally. I knew that there was nothing wrong with God. Surely if God allowed me to enter his presence and come out with the spiritual fervor and blessings to pray for family members, be an example to others and excel in spiritual gifting, surely handling my financial woes and giving me wisdom to apply to each scenario was not a hard task. In those moments, many years ago, I learned that I had an enemy who stole from me and didn't want me to have the things that God desired me to have. I had to recall that "the earth was the Lord's and the fullness thereof and they that dwell therein." I had to remind myself that if I was going to be a worshipper and equipped with power to succumb spiritual giants, then surely I can apply the same wisdom to tackle the financial giants in my life. Let me remind you of the power of a worshipper:

2 Chronicles 20:5-12, 14-23 Amplified Bible (AMP)

Jehoshaphat's Prayer

[5] Then Jehoshaphat stood in the assembly of Judah and Jerusalem, in the house of the Lord in front of the new courtyard, [6] and said, "O Lord, God of our fathers, are You not God in heaven? And do You not rule over all the kingdoms of the nations? Power and might are in Your hand, there is no one able to take a stand against You. [7] O our God, did You not drive out the inhabitants of this land before Your

people Israel and give it forever to the descendants of Your friend Abraham? [8] They have lived in it, and have built You a sanctuary in it for Your Name, saying, [9] 'If evil comes on us, or the sword of judgment, or plague, or famine, we will stand before this house and before You (for Your Name *and* Your Presence is in this house) and we will cry out to You in our distress, and You will hear and save us.' [10] Now behold, the sons of Ammon and Moab and Mount Seir, whom You would not allow Israel to invade when they came from the land of Egypt (for they turned away from them and did not destroy them), [11] here they are, rewarding us by coming to drive us out of Your possession which You have given us as an inheritance. [12] O our God, will You not judge them? For we are powerless against this great multitude which is coming against us. We do not know what to do, but our eyes are on You."

Jahaziel Answers the Prayer

[14] Then in the midst of the assembly the Spirit of the Lord came upon Jahaziel the son of Zechariah, the son of Benaiah, the son of Jeiel, the son of Mattaniah, a Levite of the sons of Asaph. [15] He said, "Listen carefully, all [you people of] Judah, and you inhabitants of Jerusalem, and King Jehoshaphat. The Lord says this to you: 'Be not afraid or dismayed at this great multitude, for the battle is not yours, but God's. [16] Go down against them tomorrow. Behold, they will come up by the ascent of Ziz, and you will find them at the end of the river valley, in front of the Wilderness of Jeruel. [17] You *need* not fight in this *battle*; take

your positions, stand and witness the salvation of the Lord who is with you, O Judah and Jerusalem. Do not fear or be dismayed; tomorrow go out against them, for the Lord is with you."'

[18] Jehoshaphat bowed with his face to the ground, and all Judah and the inhabitants of Jerusalem fell down before the Lord, worshiping Him. [19] The Levites, from the sons of the Kohathites and the sons of the Korahites, stood up to praise the Lord God of Israel, with a very loud voice.

Enemies Destroy Themselves

[20] So they got up early in the morning and went out into the Wilderness of Tekoa; and as they went out, Jehoshaphat stood and said, "Hear me, O Judah, and you inhabitants of Jerusalem! Believe *and* trust in the Lord your God and you will be established (secure). Believe *and* trust in His prophets and succeed." [21] When he had consulted with the people, he appointed those who sang to the Lord and those who praised Him in their holy (priestly) attire, as they went out before the army and said, "Praise *and* give thanks to the Lord, for His mercy *and* lovingkindness endure forever." [22] When they began singing and praising, the Lord set ambushes against the sons of Ammon, Moab, and Mount Seir, who had come against Judah; so they were struck down [in defeat]. [23] For the sons of Ammon and Moab [suspecting betrayal] rose up against the inhabitants of Mount Seir, completely

destroying them; and when they had finished with the inhabitants of Seir, they helped to destroy one another.

God is not a respecter of persons. Your praise and worship has the ability to slaughter every enemy that comes against your purpose in God! Remember, the weapons of our warfare are not carnal, but they are mighty through God, for the pulling down of strongholds! Poverty is not big or bad enough to stop the plans that God has in store for those that love the Lord and walk upright before him.

Purpose & Passion Unveils the Secrets/Strategy of the Wealthy

A man will never know if he's losing or winning, if he has not identified a clear goal in mind! A man without purpose, is bound to the pervasiveness of poverty! Proverbs 25:28 MSG – "Like a city that is broken down and without walls [leaving it unprotected] is a man who has no self-control over his spirit [and sets himself up for trouble]."

Every purpose and passion that you possess should produce P.O.W.E.R. to Get Wealth! Purpose and Passion allow a man or woman to do one thing: WHAT THEY WANT TO DO, NOT WHAT THEY HAVE TO DO! The thing about our warfare against the spirit of poverty is that it's about resources and being able to allocate them well. As a good steward of God's financial resources, we are in covenant with God's plan for our financial future and how it should impact kingdom and the lives of those we influence. I cannot tell you how many times I have done workshops and mentored individuals or couples who wanted to achieve great success in life and in their finances, but as soon as I asked them what their purpose in life was, they could not clearly communicate it. If a man or woman does not understand the reason God created them, and the assignment that their specific gifts are called to serve, then their ability to flourish in a society where most successful entrepreneurs operate out of their passion, prosperity will be diminished, if present at all! Keep in mind that we live in a capitalistic society. That means our economy thrives off of the production and exchange of goods and services. What are you willing to sell? What are you able to sell? Does the gift God gave you allow you to capture an audience where he has given you influence? Some of us are great at pushing everyone else's agenda, but have yet to identify your own. Most people yearn to connect with others who have momentum, vibrancy and have a clear understanding of the direction they desire to pursue in life. Clarity and direction are magnetic to other successful people. The reason why we are not money magnets is because you have failed to identify the place where God is looking to use you and advance his strategic kingdom agenda! Find His purpose and His plan for your life and the P.O.W.E.R. to Get Wealth will be released unto you and strategically align with other movers and shakers in your sphere of influence.

Practice Undergirds the P.O.W.E.R. of Strategic Transformation

We must understand that building wealth that is sustainable through successive generations is intentional! In order to perfect this craft, like any other skillset, we must practice! Anyone who takes the time to regularly enhance and build upon their skill sets have no choice but to become an expert or at the least knowledgeable enough to make informed decisions. That's why I stress that becoming a good steward is synonymous with the work of a personal financial manager. From monthly budgets to projects that require your financial diligence, practice builds the momentum toward taking on the responsibility of family, church and community that requires the skillset of a bonafide grade (A) personal financial manager. It was through practice that I began to look further into what methods I used to help accelerate my retirement savings, maximize income, minimize taxes and become a good steward in regard to personal debt, bills and financial responsibilities to my family and church. Once those skills were honed I began to layer in financial contributions to various community organizations including my alma mater. This was not something I learned from a mentor who took me aside and gave me all of the highs and lows of being a financial manager, but it took bumps, bruises and common sense methods along with the help of God to order my steps. A few years ago I received the assignment to be added as a trustee in my local church and I was dumbfounded. I knew that I was a faithful steward for many years in tithe and offerings, but it wasn't until I had a spiritual awakening in my prayer time where the spirit of God said, "Now, I can trust you!" My life has no longer been the same. If God can trust you financially with yourself and your family, then you can be trusted with God's church and his community! Remember my 7P's that were given to me by a former pastor, Prior-Proper-Planning-Prevents-Pitiful-Poor-Performance, so PRACTICE!

Performance Upholds P.O.W.E.R. to Get Wealth and turns Strategic Victory into Legacy

POWER IS ORGANIZED PEOPLE with ORGANIZED MONEY!!!

Now we must begin to access and make sure that we are doing everything we can to cultivate a lifestyle of wealth and wellness with the actions we take. I have listed below the steps and chronological order that I believe everyone should follow as it relates to cultivating and growing your wealth. Where do you stand as it relates to these items? Are you working toward these tasks? Have you concerned yourself with them and looking for new financial ventures to explore? Do you need to put in work to walk through these items so you can be well on your way in achieving milestones through mind, money and ministry solutions? Ultimately, we must understand that warring until you win has everything to do with the resilience it takes to no longer accept status quo excuses for the short-comings that are found in your financial health. I understand that there are occasions and instances where some of us get to skate around the pecking order that provides a roadmap to financial wellness. However, for the masses, including myself, we have worked hard to obtain our footing in a society that refuses to give anything away for free! I decided several years ago that I would do my work. I decided that my working hard was not the real ingredient that would transition me from the pit to the palace, but that my resilience to war until I won was going to ultimately serve its justice. In this journey with God, failure must not be an option! We must decide that the time we've spent working hard can be as foolish as operating blindly, without a roadmap for wealth and wellness. When you are positioned with God's plan in hand that tells you the wealth of the wicked is stored up for the righteous, then you don't have to worry about any opposition that thinks it has a chance to stand in your way! That goes for generational iniquities, DNA, race or gender inequality or any other demonic forces that think they have the final say on God's plan for your life. Resilience is the final component of P.O.W.E.R. to Get Wealth that is an intrinsic gift to those who believe in a power greater than themselves to usher them into a lifestyle that surpasses the heights of generations that have come before them. You have received the P.O.W.E.R. from your confession and commitment to taking this journey of wealth and wellness. **Now, it is time to make sure that the P.O.W.E.R. you received is not limited by religious jargon and antics that talk about a great God but diminishes its impact because of your personal challenges and inability to finish the job. Finish what you started!**

1) Establish a Budget / Disciplined Action Plan (D.A.P.)

2) Build Your Emergency Expense or Cash Reserve (Set aside 3-6 months of cash savings)

3) Work on eliminating your outstanding Debt

4) Participate in your workplace retirement plan (i.e. 401k, 403b, Solo-401k, SEP IRA)

5) Invest in Taxable Brokerage accounts or Roth IRA (if you qualify & after you are maximizing your contributions to a workplace retirement plan)

6) Investigate other opportunities for overflow & advancement (Real Estate Investing, Private Equity Purchases, Entrepreneurship & Venture Capitalist ideas, etc....)

………………..**IN THAT ORDER!!!**

CHAPTER 5

The Responsibility of the GBH

N ow is the acceptable time, to remove false burdens and false
obligations. Take the "S" off your chest; you're not JESUS and
you can't save everybody! (but you can make disciples) Each one must
teach one and not merely provide a crutch to those who are
marginalized to further impede any hope for progress or perpetuate
stereotypical behaviors that sustain black inferiority complexes and or
underachieving efforts! Layers upon layers of responsibility, whether
for your family, church or community can overwhelm any one person
that shoulders their own accomplishments to be the catalyst of change
for those who assisted in 'cultivating' their march toward success as
well those who look to them as a measuring rod for treading the same
path. From the huge entourage of the entertainer and professional
athletes to the living room full of onlookers and supporters at your
family home that root you on for the first television campaign, radio
station session or book release event that highlights your success; there

is a sense of wanting to give back to all who have helped create this monumental event in your life! Understandably so, I mean you did learn some manners or respect from your parents, grandparents or other adult mentor growing up right? Wealth should never create a crutch for others to become complacent [or milk the idea that you owe someone for your level of achievement], however it should be used as a change agent for open doors and opportunities to be maximized. The responsibility of the Great Black Hope (GBH) is one of emotional and politically charged pressure that can undo the success of any individual that falls prey to the cycle of having to take care of everything and everybody as a tribute or payback to cheerleaders or close associates of their past as a token of appreciation for their newly acquired wealth and success. From the 1st millionaire in the family or any real hint of financial stability that stands out from the majority, to the 1st college graduate, master's degree or doctor in the family, the pressure to create a path for others seems to be the sentiment of many close onlookers who strive to break the same cycles of defeat. Hang in there team! This is not a bad thing to want the very things that God created for us to enjoy, but let's remember that to whom much is given, much is required! Along with the newly found success, many times is a clear path of systemic sacrifices over an extended period of time to achieve it! The Great Black Hope (GBH) is the sacrificial lamb. You could also categorize them as the over-achiever, the highly gifted or highly motivated individual who by any means necessary, was able to chart a path of success in their profession or career and won, against all odds!

However, those that remain must understand that the positioning of this individual must be strategically crafted so there is permanence in their transitioning, then offer a path for others to celebrate and follow its directive that can be implemented in their personal pursuits for progression and prosperity! One of my favorite readings from W.E.B. Dubois, *The Talented Tenth*, gives insight to the significance of trailblazers within a community that share the responsibility of heightening the awareness of others with the understanding that their personal achievements give precedent for others to follow.

Was there ever a nation on God's fair earth civilized from the bottom upward? Never; it is, ever was and ever will be from the top downward that culture filters. The Talented Tenth rises and pulls all that are worth the saving up to their vantage ground. This is the history of human progress; and the two historic mistakes which have hindered that progress were the thinking first that no more could ever rise save the few already risen; or second, that it would be better the unrisen to pull the risen down. (Dubois, 10)

We have work to do as leaders, who are financially independent, and have been identified as the forerunners in our families, communities and churches that have the ability to infuse change for the whole. This starts with your own financial wellness and creating a pathway of success for others to follow.

Many African American households have been categorized as part of what has been labeled the "sandwich generation." These family leaders take care of primary and immediate family needs for both spouse and children, but also bear the burden of extended family members (parents, grandchildren, aunts, uncles, cousins, etc). Some of us may be first generation college graduates or successful first generation entrepreneurs that bear the responsibility of bringing the rest of the family to the next level. Even those who have a history of post-graduate education in the family, professional athletes or entertainers can't seem to shake the cycle of an impoverished mentality due to overspending (due to your newly found success or celebration of your latest achievement) or simply over-extending yourself to resolve the needs of others. There are a few things the GBH needs to understand so as to ensure they are using wealth and wellness wisdom practices in order to effect change in the lives of those you love. Ask yourself the following questions to gauge your level of involvement in resolving the needs of others around you:

1) Is this my assignment?

    A. If so, proceed with love, patience, wisdom & understanding. Remember, however, your goal is to be a guide, not a crutch. Make sure any investment you make from this point, is financially sound and full of wisdom, for both parties involved.

    B. If not, you may need to refer them to a professional help service. Also take the time to assess why you may be targeted as the "go to" person to resolve everyone else's financial woes.

2) What emotions are tied to being the 'Great Black Hope' (GBH) in your family?

    A. The urge to feel needed or feel some sort of relevance that stems from others needing or depending upon your stability

    B. False Burdens / False Obligations – many who have been identified as the life-saver, lifeguard, coach, and promoter of good in the family often wear the hat of false burdens and obligations. This person legitimately wants to see the well-being of others in their family manifest, however, some are not willing to do or forego what is needed to sustain their wealth & wellness journey.

    C. Fatigue? Exhaustion? When does the urge to feel needed or relevant turn into frustration, fatigue and exhaustion……due to being over-extended, under-appreciated, used & abused, etc.…

3) Identify what the issue "really" is with the family member who needs your financial assistance. (i.e. is their financial stress due to lack of employment, mismanagement, addiction, lack of direction or in identifying passion to be pursued, etc…)

4) Identify if you are equipped to help resolve the issue (i.e. some issues take counseling, strategic long-term plans, finances, training, etc…)

5) What is the plan of action? Someone has to take an initiative to decide what is needed to add value or empower the person in

their circumstance so it doesn't become a recurring situation or financial burden on you & your immediate family for the long haul.

6) Make an agreement as to how performance or growth will be monitored.

(i.e. will positive growth allow the person to transition into their next phase of life, financial guidance, stewardship, etc...) If you don't take time to measure performance, you leave the door open to revert back into financial mismanagement and poor habits that created the initial problem!

The bottom line is, although many of us may think we are doing well and have successful careers, savings, investments, real estate and other perks that show our ability to adapt and excel on numerous levels, the financial status and security of the GBH is not indicative of the whole. What God wants us to understand as a community is that YOU may be doing okay, but WE are not doing well at all!

Let us look to the word for guidance and see what it says concerning individual prosperity vs. the state of the community for the believers...

Haggai 1:2-10 (AMP)

[2] "Thus says the Lord of hosts: 'These people say, "The time has not come that the Lord's house (temple) should be [a]rebuilt."' [3] Then the word of the Lord came by Haggai the prophet, saying, [4] "Is it time

for you yourselves to live in your [expensive] paneled houses while this house [of the Lord] lies in ruins?" [5] Now therefore, thus says the Lord of hosts, "Consider your ways *and* thoughtfully reflect on your conduct! [6] You have planted much, but you harvest little; you eat, but you do not have *enough*; you drink, but you do not have *enough* to be intoxicated; you clothe yourselves, but no one is warm *enough*; and he who earns wages earns them *just to put* them in a bag with holes in it [because God has withheld His blessing]."

[7] Thus says the Lord of hosts, "Consider your ways *and* thoughtfully reflect on your conduct! [8] Go up to the hill country, bring lumber and rebuild My house (temple), that I may be pleased with it and be glorified," says the Lord [accepting it as done for My glory]. [9] You look for much [harvest], but it comes to little; and even when you bring that home, I blow it *away*. Why?" says the Lord of hosts. "Because of My house, which lies in ruins while each of you runs to his own house [eager to enjoy it]. [10] Therefore, because of you [that is, your sin and disobedience] the heavens withhold the dew and the earth withholds its produce.

God, through the prophet, makes clear that the state of the temple reflects the state of the community; both lie in ruins, despite isolated signs of individual prosperity in the community. Without a solidifying center (i.e., the temple, for Haggai), the community can exert all the effort it wants, but to no avail in a culture of self-serving shallowness, material goods; from food to clothing, will not suffice. The fact that you're doing good is not bad in the sight of God. The goal is to understand that as a leader and catalyst of change, within your family, church and community, that the GBH must remain present and willing to help others who are less fortunate than themselves. That doesn't mean you provide a crutch for them to continue in what may be bad behavior or lack of knowledge, but to do your part as a contributor and cultivator of good!

I have a family member who called me to ask to borrow money. At one point they would call on a regular basis. I invited that individual to sit with me and go through a budget and overview of their finances so that we could identify areas for improvement and have them well on their way to achieving a wealth and wellness lifestyle. The arrangement was to meet with me first, and then I would give them the money that they needed to resolve their financial woes. They recanted their request due to their lack of involvement in their own financial future! I have never received additional phone calls from that person again for money because they now understand if I choose to help a situation it will be on my terms and not theirs! Understand, as the GBH in your family, you have been afforded an opportunity to help others, but everyone will not receive the instructions you give them in order for change to be implemented. While we are chipping away at other people's debts and sharing or bearing the responsibility of the burdens we didn't create, we must remember, "The rich ruleth over the poor, and the borrower is servant to the lender." (Proverbs 22:7) There may be times when you can help. But there may be other times when you cannot help. The burden of resolving everyone else's financial obligations should not be solely upon your shoulders. What must be communicated is that if you don't have a handle on this situation and a plan of resolution for empowerment, it will extend an invitation for excuses! Do we all have some family or friends that may need help at some time or another, of course! But what we cannot allow is to let any outside influences shape how, when and in what capacity we deal with our own financial obligations to immediate family. If it gets to where I'm paying my bills late to pay yours on time or help you play catch-up, then I'm really not positioned well to extend help. I must hit on this subject because so many times we say in the church that people are robbing Peter, to pay Paul. This is only true in the cases of those who have not allowed themselves sufficient time for growth and development into a place of financial maturity prior to going back to extend a helping hand. I tell people all the time when assisting clients with a budget, the numbers don't lie. They tell a story and create a picture on their own. If you're not ready to bear the responsibility of others then you must abort the request to be Superman in someone's financial storm of life.

The image of the person who carries the responsibility of the GBH can be misleading. Many seem to want to always ask or target you as their personal lender when you dress nice, drive nice and have possessions that others only dream of obtaining. That's why I pride myself on making people understand my journey and my story. My journey and lifestyle of wealth and wellness is a life-long pursuit. The things I possess are only an indication of my diligence toward God's agenda as a steward. We must share our testimonies of faith and overcoming to others who face financial struggle that they too can break the cycle of defeat, lack and poverty in their lives. We achieve milestones in our finances and break the curse of poverty through mind, money and ministry solutions! The mind has to be changed then the money will follow! Many times I had to deny myself even though others thought I was spending a lot of money on clothing or other possessions. I love to present myself well. First impressions are lasting impressions; however, I will never take the opportunity to elevate my outward appearance above opportunities to maintain good stewardship.

The life of the GBH is a tough one – it's a life of a servant, but it's also the life of a judge!

If you have been identified by God to target the goals of your family as well provide focus, discipline and a plan of action to achieve those objectives, then you must possess a spirit of DISCERNMENT! You have to know when you are being conned, and know when God needs you to be a resource/gateway to walking into new prosperity! Remember God sees and knows the mantle of prosperity is upon you…..so does the DEVIL! Random people who mean you no good will approach you with their plans to succeed in life and want you to be their lifetime advocate, investor and capital campaign manager but lack the substance, discipline and integrity to achieve wealth and wellness, God's way! I can be your coach and help pull you out of the pit, but you may not be positioned for prosperity and overflow. I can only speak to you the way God has given it to me. I will not feed you a watered-down version of my transition into P.O.W.E.R.! God wants his servants to not only walk in spiritual authority, but also as financiers in the kingdom and in the earth! You can't walk in that authority if you're not willing to call a fraudulent person out on their foolishness. This level of discernment will save you plenty of headaches down the road and a lot of money from being squandered in fruitless investments. Just as you examine various investment options for future returns and dividends, you must also examine people who have no purpose and no plans for achieving their desired outcome in life! A bad investment is simply that; on paper, or in person! Have you been identified as the Joseph (strategic kingdom planner) in your family? If so, you must know which season to sow versus save. Even in seasons that were 'lean' Joseph was able to glean. Understand what various seasons mean and how they impact you personally, within your family and within your community! The GBH has been anointed to see in advance and ahead of time because of the strategic and prophetic vision you have for others that are a part of the package deal as a servant leader. What does the GBH see for entrepreneurial endeavors personally, within his or her community, and church? You are able to call forth entrepreneurial endeavors that will change your life and the world of those who dare to share your sphere of influence! Money doesn't go far when you have to use assets to support multiple households or extended family due to being the GBH and cultivator of change in your family, church and community. Remember, the numbers don't lie and the picture will tell the story. I have experienced this on more than a few occasions and trust me this can become a major obstacle toward your goals of achieving **P.O.W.E.R. to Get Wealth!**

The GBH has to be a GREAT COMMUNICATOR!

The GBH has to learn how to be a great communicator within your family or sphere of influence. That means you are now challenged with opportunities to create various methods of learning that invoke open dialogue, comfort and different levels of understanding when attempting to walk others in your family toward financial independence. Remember, you are not obligated to be a crutch, but God has designed you to be a light. Light does several things. It brings revelation – being able to identify where you are; it brings illumination – incorporating a plan of action to clarify objectives for milestones to be achieved; and it brings experimentation – giving others the opportunity to exercise and implement personal strategic plans for financial independence and tracking progress.

Matthew 5:16 says, "Let your light so shine before men, that they may see your good works, and glorify your Father which is in heaven." When Glory for all that you have achieved and accomplished is given back to God first, he will continue to strategically align your motivations and your manifestations of his goodness to encourage others and be the guiding light to their own pursuit of financial independence.

CHAPTER 6

For the "Good of the House!"

———◆——◯——◆———

"For the Good of the House" is a communal slogan used in the setting of a Morehouse Alumni meeting, used to foster brotherly bonds and solicit support for endeavors that impact both the individual and community in a productive and transformative way. Using this slogan is a continuation of the bonds that bind and forge greater opportunities for communal change and resistance.

When we begin to dig into many of the issues that surround minority communities and the subjects of finance, poverty, stewardship, financial literacy and wellness, many of the obstacles that have surfaced in the past still haunt our future. These obstacles are relative to communal distractions and divisions that plague our communities. When we look at the mortgage crisis of 2008 and its correlation with predatory lending practices, minority communities were hit the hardest! Our communities and families lost homes and everything they worked hard to build because we put our trust in a system that has always favored the lender over the borrower (Prov. 22:7).

The truth in the matter is when are we going to wake up about how we spend our money? On many occasions we have refused to support African-American institutions of religion, professional support services or education. As well, we cater to a capitalistic economy that glorifies debt, big-spending and materialistic goods that threaten the sustainability of our community! You may say, "why would I think our spending actually hinders our community and prevents growth, shouldn't it boost the economy?" Well, not when the money you spend is not circulating within our educational systems, our religious organizations and our medical and professional help facilities. We are fighting a losing war considering that many of us start behind the curve as it relates to disposable income and education. Comparative analyses prove that African-Americans lag behind other major race groups up to almost a 30% income deficit when comparing equal education and experience to their white counterparts.

Another housekeeping item that needs to be addressed is the impact of education and income as it relates to minority participation in workplace retirement plans. Ariel Investments, a major mutual fund provider with over $13 billion dollars in assets under management, conducts an annual black investor survey which highlights several key components that impact saving and investing in the African-American community in comparison to White Americans. Many employers who strategically investigate the results of employee-participation surveys as it relates to minority savings goals and active involvement in its company sponsored retirement plans show the alarming trends of lagging participation rates that are directly correlated to dispersion of income amongst major race groups. Workplace retirement plans are seen as a key entry point for African-Americans into the market. According to Ariel's Black Investor Survey, seven out of ten African-American investors cite workplace retirement plans as a contributing reason for becoming an investor – double the rate of the next most common reason – having extra cash on hand they wanted to grow. (Ariel Website, retrieved on 02/15/18) The bottom line is that many of us fail to exemplify the discipline it takes to invest in the stock market or other revenue generating business initiatives that can have the ability to fast track you into a lifestyle of wealth and wellness. Could it be that a lack of disposable income and cash reserves are directly correlated to missing key opportune moments to invest into the stock market for minorities? For those who fall into this category, one of the primary ways of entering into the market and growing savings at an accelerated rate is by participation in your workplace retirement plan. For some others who participate in some sort of retirement plan (401k, 403B, SEP IRA, etc.) and already strategically invest outside of those retirement options understand the power of capital gains that far outpace traditional savings methods and options available at your local bank. The willingness to forego consumption today, while targeting strategic plans to build wealth, impacts you personally and influences everyone and everything around you! And Blacks are currently more optimistic about the economy and the stock market than are whites. This optimism coupled with potential market entry through workplace retirement plans might make the coming years a unique window of opportunity to encourage more African-Americans to participate in one of the greatest wealth-generating mechanisms this country has to offer: the stock market (Ariel Investor Survey). Research from the Ariel Investor Survey also revealed a high level of education is also a predictor for African-Americans being in the market. Blacks with a graduate degree have a 72% participation rate, as compared to college graduates and below who participate at a rate of 63%.

My job is not to harp upon the specific injustices and social evils that we confront in these United States of America, but to provide a solution for best practice that can be implemented as a work-around for those who still aim to maximize opportunities in education, their profession and lifestyle goals. I know you wanted me to read you a prayer or solely dig deep into the statistics of the economic injustices we face as a community. I will provide you the information but I don't want you to use it as an excuse to diminish your progress! Ultimately, if we want our communities to thrive and our children and professional organizations to compete with the best in the world, we must begin to love ourselves and our community enough to invest within its walls and use self-love as the momentum and catalyst to make our imprint within all nations around the world! Other major race groups understand this proposal. They establish collaborative efforts to ensure that goals are met within their community first, and then they share abroad. Even when we study the community of believers in the book of Acts (early church), we understand that it was imperative that everyone understood the strength of the community flourished under the guidance of one vision, one accord and that all were going to participate. In other words communal partnerships were a key indicator in the sustainability of the entire community and in global missions to impact the world! However, they also understood that love began at home then spread abroad. (Acts 1:8) If you chose not to participate in advancing the cause of the community, then it was conceived that you were a threat to the whole and actions were taken to relieve you of your duties.

All of the professional financial gurus continue to say the same thing! Financial independence, literacy and wellness are a behavioral science. It becomes better and self-sustaining the more you implement good habits! No longer is this a cat and mouse game of chasing that aggressive stock that was mentioned to you by your co-worker while out to lunch and finding the nearest financial advisor to see what is the hot stock of the day or week, it is a game of diligence and monitoring of behaviors that are being strategically aligned to form habits of wealth and wellness goals.

Communal Touch

"The Visible Community", a train of thought introduced by theologian, Dietrich Bonhoeffer suggests a communal paradigm for (parable) being the salt of the earth; Bonhoeffer suggests quite a few strong scenarios of likening the work of discipleship to that of salt. This responsibility ultimately sheds light on either the existence or the demise of the believer. So is the existence and life of the community. If we all don't share an internal communal instinct that reverences our past, our present and our future – for the sake of shared responsibility, mobility and succession -- our demise is sure to come!

What does the story of Nehemiah say about communal touch or communal responsibility? (Dangers of Division - Nehemiah 1-5) The threat of poverty cannot exist in a connected community. It only has the ability to materialize and flourish in environments where division persists and individualistic ideologies trump the purpose, passion and progression of the whole. A divided house cannot stand! A healthy community is the direct result of healthy individuals and healthy organizations. P.O.W.E.R. is the result of organized money and organized people coming together for the sake of shared responsibility to address issues that impede the progress of the whole or share strategy that strengthens its vigor.

SUCCESS IS THE OPTIMAL RESULT OF PLANNED ENERGY AND RESOURCES THAT ARE FOCUSED!

In comparison, economic expansion and empowerment will always foster fruitful and sustaining communities because of its ability to educate, connect and uphold principles that validate the whole.

What does the story of the early church in the Book of Acts say about communal touch and responsibility, and how its lessons provide a narrative for how African-Americans can strengthen the bonds of its community today? (Distractions of Materialism – Acts 5)

THE STORY OF ANANIAS & SAPPHIRA

The story of Ananias and Sapphira is found in Acts 5, and it is a sad story, indeed. It actually begins at the end of chapter 4 with the description of the early church in Jerusalem, a group of believers so filled with the Holy Spirit that they were of one heart and one mind. Great power and grace were on the apostles, who preached and testified of the risen Savior. So knit together were the hearts of the people that they held all their possessions loosely and willingly shared them with one another, not because they were coerced but because they loved one another. Those who sold land and houses gave of their profits to the apostles, who distributed the gifts to those in need.

Two members of this group were Ananias and his wife, Sapphira; they also had sold a field. Part of the profit from their sale was kept back by the couple, and Ananias only laid a part of the money at the apostles' feet. However, Ananias made a pretense of having given *all* the proceeds. This hypocritical show may have fooled some, but not Peter, who was filled with the power of the Holy Spirit. Peter knew instantly that Ananias was lying—not just to him but to God—and exposed his hypocrisy then and there. Ananias fell down and died. When Sapphira showed up, she, too, lied to Peter and to God, saying that they had donated the *entire* proceeds of the sale of the land to the church. When her lie had been exposed, she also fell down and died at Peter's feet.

We have been told in the church that this story is primarily about lying to God and the consequences of God's judgment. I would like to present another synopsis of the text that allows us to dig further into God's revealed word as it relates to community and shared vision. When we approach this story from multi-faceted lenses, we must understand the early church was a strong communal entity within itself. This community took great pride in being a place where they experienced great successes TOGETHER. Even at the onset of the text in chapters 1 and 2, we celebrate victory together in the upper room and the outpouring of God's Holy Spirit as a SHARED experience that catapulted its community into instantaneous economic, spiritual and exponential growth! When we examine the story of Ananias and Sapphira, we must consider that in this historical setting, spiritual fervor was not the only parameter for judgment by God and the community, but there was also a strong emphasis on SHARED COMMUNAL VALUES AND RESPONSIBILITIES. In other words, we solely focused our attention on the thought of Ananias and Sapphira lying to God, when in conjunction to the lies, there was a LACK OF SHARED COMMUNAL VALUE AND RESPONSIBILITY that caused discord and disdain amongst the brethren and with God. God was not satisfied with this juncture then, and I believe that any hint of discord and lack of communal responsibility amongst its citizens always leave the door open for Satan to attack the family, community and legacy of African-Americans.

What does the story of Haggai say about the people and communal touch/responsibility? Distractions of Materialism (Haggai 1 / Acts 5)

Individual prosperity in the midst of impoverishment is no sign of God's blessing but merely a symptom of a dysfunctional, dying community! God is not concerned about personal progression in the midst of a languishing community! While individual homes prospered, the temple, the community's source and center, languished, reflecting a scandalous level of self-serving indifference to the community's well-being.

What are the results of a community that has been devastated by ISOLATION and a SELF-CENTERED Consciousness? Dilemmas of Hopelessness (Prov. 13:12; 15:22)

The Bible emphatically declares that hope deferred makes the heart sick! Waiting too long for anything can become at the very least, uncomfortable, and even worse, a source of dejection. This is why Poverty has stronger correlations with suicide rates than does unemployment or foreclosures. This study was documented in 2016 by UCLA. No wonder many of our brothers and sisters in low-income communities struggle with giving accolades to others alongside them who seem to make it out of the cycle of socio-economic inequalities that have left battle wounds and mental scarring strong enough to intoxicate three generations of single black mothers looking for answers but in all the wrong places. No wonder we take the minimal earnings that we get and either reduce them to the victory of securing another Gucci belt or at least a knock-off version that resembles the slightest hope of achievement in a battle fought with tears, misunderstanding, lack of mobility, and lack of education opportunities. You just get tired! This responsibility of socio-economic status and victory, was never supposed to be achieved through the efforts of individuals. It takes a community!

Communal Responsibility

Why is it that African-Americans seem to be the only race group/class that struggle with internalized cannibalism when sustaining higher levels of professional or economic success, only to horde amongst themselves opportunities and rights among people that should be shared, "FOR THE GOOD OF THE HOUSE"! When we examine the stories of Ananias and Sapphira, it starkingly contrasts that of the story of Barnabas in the previous chapter (Acts 4:36-37), where he sold a field that belonged to him, then brought the money, and laid it at the apostles' feet. The contrast between Barnabas and Ananias and Sapphira underscores the importance of sharing one's possessions as a barometer of the disciple's relationship with God's spirit. In the same manner, we are confronted with opportunities to support and extend the reach and impact of our communities and similar to Ananias and Sapphira, make self-centered choices that subvert our relationship with God.

Aaron Hurst, Founder and President of the Taproot Foundation, is widely known for his thought-leadership in social responsibility. He says, "To thrive, we must learn, earn and return throughout our careers." In order for our communities to remain vibrant and maintain its impact into further generations, there must be a willingness to share, develop and accelerate from within. The primary responsibility of this task belongs to the GBH and others who are committed to the task of making our communities great again!

An excerpt from 'Learning As a Way of Leading' by Stephen Brookfield, says:

First, community is impossible without ongoing communication. Part of the rationale for building community is to provide a setting for exchanging experiences, knowledge, and ideas, a setting where competing visions of what people desire can be hashed out. Continuing communication among the members of a community helps bring them closer together and bind them to a shared purpose. Second, people who are part of a community give up some of their individual identity to identify with the whole. They literally commune or join with others in pursuit of something that is greater than themselves. They do this because they know that community can accomplish goals and impart new meanings to experience in ways that cannot be achieved individually. …..any common vision that is developed is designed to promote the common good of all. Community brings us back to the idea that whatever benefits an individual should be regarded as something for all to enjoy.

Community is the power of collective thought and action, demonstrating how much more can be accomplished in a cohesive group than can be done by a lone individual. We learn to create community because of its potential for stimulating actions that can transform the balance of power within the larger society. By virtue of numbers and collective strength, community solidarity enables people to exert pressure on the powerful few to redistribute resources, share authority and actualize democracy. (Brookfield, 191-194)

Alienation and separatist ideas within black communities have minimalized the impact of its spending power. This reality speaks to the notion of blacks being disregarded due to the lack of momentum and socio-economic influence that they have on other race groups. We are regarded as big spenders, not big contributors or big savers.

According to the most recent Nielsen Consumer reports, African Americans' spending power reached $1.2 trillion in 2017 and is predicted to increase to $1.4 trillion by 2020. This would typically mean there is a significant level of importance that should be targeted toward connecting with African-American consumers. However, shopping trends and consumer behavior are distinctly different from other major race groups. Nevertheless, our ability to organize for the greater good does rear its head at times which shows our potential to impact and influence global economies as well reemphasize the notion that our community is not to be dismissed when considering our collective spending power and its reach. H&M clothing found this out rather quickly when they decided to have a young black boy wear a sweatshirt depicting a monkey in its marketing campaign. It's not absolutely certain that there was any malice intent to instigate race relations within the African-American community, but I believe it was in poor judgment to execute such a marketing campaign in light of the race relations that exist within the United States of America.

Sustainability and generational wealth is challenged due to the threat of immediate gratification versus developing new patterns for wealth accumulation and building of wealth transformation habits. When one community fails to "take care of the house", each successive generation bears the responsibility of rebuilding its walls from inception, on top of a system that is already broken and desolate! The church has been the fabric of our communities for centuries, and instead of forcing you to study every scripture based around giving and stewardship, I need you to use your energy on extracting the vital resources and lessons that were the focus for which the texts were written.

When we talk about community activity and the strength that comes from a sense of shared values, we don't talk anymore about GENERATIONAL INHERITANCE!

- Who passes down inheritances anymore?

- Do African Americans possess any shared beliefs that highlight historical significance or value? (recall the story of the King Children where Rev. Bernice King had to have a court order issued against her sibling brothers to stop them from auctioning off her father, Dr. Martin Luther King, Jr.'s, personal bible! You could have the Nobel Peace Prize for museum display, even some of the notes, but his personal bible? Do we hold on to anything that has historical significant value? Or at least position its use to maximize efficiency or creating a learning opportunity for the community he served at-large, not for personal financial gain.

- Why do we sell all of our possessions? Our land, our history, our ideologies, our recipes, etc….

- Where are the sons & daughters who cherish the inheritance that blessed them along the way and are ready to make sacrifices to extend its reach and impact to global communities?

Communal Fires (The Threat of Poverty.....and fear of going back to save others)

Communal Fires deals with the threats that lurk within our communities that we fail to put to rest because of our lack of knowledge, experience or the fear of succumbing to that very issue that has created problems for many. Poverty is an epidemic that affects our nation and our world. However, the conversation of financial literacy within African American communities has been one that was avoided all together because of the history of a people in these United States. Why talk about financial well-being when we are dealing with crisis from slavery, to Jim Crow and now cultural genocide of people who for a long time were targeted simply because of the color of their skin? Nevertheless, the triumph of minority communities to survive in the wake of race relations in this country and to become major contributors to its evolution and sustainability and overall success is worth talking about!

Where do we begin in conversation? There is a great undertaking we still have yet to achieve as a community, where there are great social evils that still persist in presenting obstacles to the advancement of minority persons, however, our fear of moving forward will be the only obstacle that stands a chance in this heightened day of awareness, social media, and other communication mediums that drive our culture today. Poverty is not based upon how much money we make on our jobs or our ability to systematically save or redirect those funds into other wealth building opportunities. Poverty is a distorted mindset that hinders a person from the ability to identify trouble spots in their finances, implement strategy to enforce change, and then monitor progress as a measuring rod of sustainability and transformative wealth practice.

The troubling thought persists as it relates to the economic sustainability of an entire community to care enough to expand our walls and reach, yet maintain a barometer of sensitivity in establishing procedures and policies to piggyback the failing efforts of those less fortunate. In other words, we FEAR GOING BACK TO SAVE OTHERS!

For many of the communal fires that exist, the THREAT OF POVERTY AND THE FEAR OF GOING BACK TO SAVE OTHERS, is a direct result of post traumatic slave syndrome referenced by Dr. Joy DeGruy that also tie into the economic growth and sustainability of our communities as a whole. Dr. Na'im Akbar made references to how African-Americans struggle to support one another because we were historically pitted against one another for survival in 'Breaking the Chains of Psychological Slavery'. He also tied these historical acts of being pitted against one another as a type of communal fire that impede community progress due to negative internalized self-consciousness behaviors that impact our religion, leadership and finances within a community.

So how do we get our families and our community focused on being with 'One Accord?' Take the opportunity to discuss the statements or questions below and write down what you feel presents safeguards or obstacles to your achieving household goals with one accord!

1) What do you do when you & your spouse are not on the same page about finances?

2) When do to apply for joint credit versus separate?

3) Are having separate accounts ever a good idea?

4) Why should everyone be building the House?

5) Why should everyone be contributing toward the goal of financial confidence & independence for the family?

These are the conversations and stories that we need to have in order to better appreciate the story of Ananias and Sapphira, Nehemiah and Haggai and the communal significance attached to the responsibility of sharing in times of need while utilizing our personal stewardship to advance the community! In the height of the greatest economic expansion and professional opportunities afforded to minority individuals, many of our communities suffer because of our inability to SEIZE & SHARE! Please understand that while communicating and sharing some of our greatest victories and triumphs as a community, there is still a great undertaking we still have yet to achieve as a community. There are great social evils that still persist in presenting obstacles to the advancement of minority persons and the objectives we look to achieve within our communities, our faith, educational institutions and professional help organizations. However, we must learn to seize the moments that present themselves and be sure to maximize those moments to foster environments where we share responsibilities, share our victories and rejoice together in triumph! Take the opportunity to seize and share information, For the Good of the House!

CHAPTER 7

Get in the Game!

W e cannot rest upon the laurels of complacency and a BIC (Black Inferiority Complex), thinking that injustice and inequality will hide its ugly head. It's time for the Game Changers to rise up!! Aren't you tired of accepting the status quo? Don't you ever get disappointed with not being able to provide your family the best opportunities to sharpen their competitive advantages in the marketplace? Proverbs 20:4 MSG, says, "A farmer too lazy to plant in the spring has nothing to harvest in the fall." You can't get ahead of the game, if you're not already in the game. Many of us go from year to year internalizing what it takes to get started and never bring those thoughts into fruition. Every playing field has its own set of rules. Learn the game in the field where you have an interest in developing a career or building a business….then change it to work in your favor!

Getting in the Game heightens the possibility of your achieving success and creating a wealth and wellness lifestyle for you and your family. A lot of us think that frequent social media postings and likes of our candid photo shoots that display expensive clothes, cars and other high ticket items validate our entrance and sustainability in a lifestyle of wealth and wellness, but it is quite the contrary! Surveys show that many of the wealthiest individuals have spending habits that are opposite of the portrait displayed through various social media channels. As well many of those same wealthy individuals target the same wealth-generating practices that propel them further into financial independence that has the ability to be sustained for generations.

We introduced the idea of developing a Disciplined Action Plan (DAP) in chapter one to cover the essentials of budgeting our finances and embarking on a new journey in wealth and wellness. Now, we need to examine the parameters of our personal habits and hobbies that contribute to excessive spending and mismanagement that hinder us from *Getting in the Game*!

If you're going to become a game changer in your family, church, community and essentially your sphere of influence/professional expertise, there are (5) essential questions you must be able to answer regarding readiness for reward?

1) What is your Metron or area of influence (professional passion for provision) and how are you developing it for next level service?

2) Are you willing to make sacrifices to share your Metron (professional passion for provision) with your family, your church, your community and the world?

3) Do you have a 3-5 year progressive plan of exposing, sharing and communicating your passion to a selective audience? i.e. family, community, church, network, targeted-client base, etc…

4) Have you identified the essential components of your "Professional Passion for Provision" plan and how they make you distinctly different from your peers or others that share a similar passion?

5) Have you asked God to enlarge your territory in this field of expertise as well provide guidance on the plan he has for you impacting others in the capacity to produce faith, finance & future progression?

So as we are discussing key items that need to be addressed in order for you to strategically maneuver your place of provision and positioning yourself to get in the game, we must understand the dynamics of the marketplace, corporate workspace or the area of influence that God has given you to make provision for your family, church and community.

What is the Marketplace or the Game Location?

The place of exchange, where sharing of information and ideas on common ground come together in collaboration of your **METRON** (area of influence & expertise) and **THE MARKETPLACE** (the arena of competitive or commercial dealings; the world of trade) that positions your **MONEY to be MAXIMIZED** and the **MINSTRY OF JESUS to be MAGNIFIED!** In the marketplace…..unbelievers take Christians as a joke, because our money is a joke! In the marketplace, unbelievers who respect your profession, and your money, have the ability to respect your God! There is a new epidemic impacting the Body of Christ, especially our young people that insists on luring our seed and this generation away from the church…all for the love of MONEY and FAME!

The lie has been told that there is no prosperity in the church….you can't love God and be prosperous also! You can't live a life for God and be a multi-millionaire…..you can't be saved, sanctified and be a BOSS! People are looking for "FIRST CLASS FAITH"! No longer do I want to be associated with a God that can minister to my SELF-WORTH, but unable to produce NET-WORTH!

Psalm 35:27 says:

"Let them shout for joy, and be glad, that favor my righteous cause; yea, let them say continually, let the Lord be MAGNIFIED, which hath pleasure in the prosperity of his servant."

Conversations are birthed out of a place called familiarity!

What I have learned in my professional experience in the marketplace is that people may not understand your background or who you are as an individual, but your drive and professional astuteness will open the door for your being positioned for next level! It's not about how hard you work, but knowing that you are strategically aligning yourself with good people, good character, good opportunities, and good skillsets that can propel you into greatness!

It takes money, to make money. What we have to understand about finance is that our ultimate goal in securing our finances and the future of our families and all those we love (church, community) is attributed to how well we manage, or become stewards over the things that God has placed in our hands to make provision for us. One of the first opportunities to demonstrate great stewardship over God's provision in your life is thru your ability to handle your finances and manage your livable wages, applying the 4-Quadrant Lifestyle (see Chapter 1) to Wealth and Wellness principles.

As mentioned before, average 401k balances for African-Americans and Hispanics lag behind in participation rates and contributions in comparison to their white and Asian counterparts.

Let's keep it real here. Much of this has to do with the widening gap of socio-economic inequalities that are exploited through income disparities amongst race groups. However, there is still a huge component that the African-American community has to confront, which is the lack of discipline and integrity in handling our finances that is an extension of mismanagement, poor habits and lack of knowledge. The current maximum allowable employee deferral contribution to a 401k plan for 2018 is $18,500 (for employees under the age of 50). This does not take into consideration the employer's match to the plan during the same calendar year. Several studies regarding employer participation done by Ariel Funds as well Prudential show that African Americans, even if they participate in 401(k) and other retirement accounts, have a median savings amount that is more than 50% less in their employer-sponsored plans in comparison to the general population.

Let's do the math. This would mean in today's world, the average employee has the option to do a maximum contribution to their employer-sponsored retirement plan of $18,500. In a 5-year period, that would provide an excess of $90,000 of retirement savings. Considering the average 401(k) balance of African-Americans fall well below $90,000 in retirement savings lets me know that we are definitely not taking advantage of maxing out the retirement savings option. So let's use conservative numbers to provide an illustration.

Example 1 of Annual Savings to a 401k Plan

Let's use and average annual salary of $50k @ 5% pre-tax contribution rate

$50,000 x 5% = $2,500 annual savings

5yr of savings @ 5% contribution rate = $12,500

10yrs of savings @ 5% contribution rate = $25,000

20yrs of savings @ 5% contribution rate = $50,000

As we know, these numbers are conservative, and also don't consider any growth or rates of return in the market, however there are many who still fall below the average salary sample that will essentially cause this number to be lower at the 5-year and 10-year savings goals. Even for an individual at the same average annual salary rate of $50,000 who only saves $1,000 annually into some sort of savings or investment vehicle, not considering investment performance, should have in the neighborhood of $5,000 at 5yrs, $10,000 at 10yrs, and $20,000 at 20 years. Saving $1,000 over a year only equates to setting aside an amount of either $20 weekly or $80 monthly.

So my question to many of us is, why are you in a profession for 10 or 20 years, providing service to an employer that still has not allowed you to save what is an average of only $1,000 of annual savings to a savings or retirement vehicle of your choice? LACK OF DISCIPLINE, FEAR and lack of knowledge!

So what about some others who actually make higher incomes and have access to greater levels of disposable income? Do you know that African-Americans in 2017 exceeded a collective annual spending power of $1 trillion dollars?

Example 2 of Annual Savings to a 401k Plan

Let's use an average annual salary of $100k @ 5% pre-tax contribution rate

$100,000 x 5% = $5,000 annual savings

5yr of savings @ 5% contribution rate = $25,000

10yrs of savings @ 5% contribution rate = $50,000

20yrs of savings @ 5% contribution rate = $100,000

That means many of us may have access to higher incomes but we face the same apparent obstacles if your average does not trend close or higher than the examples provided. LACK OF DISCIPLINE, FEAR and lack of knowledge have been obstacles to your creating a lifestyle of wealth and wellness for your family!

Whether you have a larger annual income that you're able to work with or a smaller annual income, the solution is still the same in order to build your wealth! Your level of DISCIPLINE must be in order! When we practice these habits regularly and begin to implement debt elimination, taxable investments, and insurance products, etc…then our money will allow us to explore greater opportunities to create wealth that are typically only accessible to more sophisticated investors!

"Never let people, places or things occupy you for extended lengths of time and it not be worth your while – it is equivalent to letting a strongman or a thief into your house, who has spoiled and plundered your goods!"

Principles produce prosperity! If you learn how to drive (safety being your end resolve), considering all things, traffic laws, speed and good defensive driving, it doesn't matter if you're driving a Kia Rio, Honda Accord, Mercedes Benz, or Bentley GT Convertible. When the principles of driving are applied, you will arrive to your destination safely! The same logic can be applied to principles and disciplines that produce prosperity as you layer in strategic principles for implementation, you'll begin to produce a harvest!

Now let's be honest here. The examples we used to illustrate savings levels at 5, 10 and 20 years are extremely conservative. They don't consider inflation rates, growth nor the fact that most people need to save 10-15% annually, of their income to retire comfortably. God's economic plan for prosperity sets you up for a disciplined life! The reason why some of you can't stand to see yourself saving 10% annually is because you can barely part with the first 10% that goes to the church (Tithe). When you learn to part with the first 10%, God will condition you on how to deal with the rest so that your labor and rewards work for you in the long term!

If you are not building some level of experience in your profession or skillset that allows you to advance in areas of personal finance, then you have no point of reference from which to target your passion for progression! Whether you are an employee, self-employed person or business owner, identifying those skillsets that differentiate or highlight marketable qualities for sale or growth target is key!

Now let's look further into what God is saying to us as we aspire to "Get in the Game". Matthew 25:14-30 teaches us about the Parable of the Talents.

The Parable of the Talents

[14] "For it will be like a man going on a journey, who called his servants[k] and entrusted to them his property. [15] To one he gave five talents,[s] to another two, to another one, to each according to his ability. Then he went away. [16] He who had received the five talents went at once and traded with them, and he made five talents more. [17] So also he who had the two talents made two talents more. [18] But he who had received the one talent went and dug in the ground and hid his master's money. [19] Now after a long time the master of those servants came and settled accounts with them. [20] And he who had received the five talents came forward, bringing five talents more, saying, 'Master, you delivered to me five talents; here, I have made five talents more.' [21] His master said to him, 'Well done, good and faithful servant.[s] You have been

faithful over a little; I will set you over much. Enter into the joy of your master.'²² And he also who had the two talents came forward, saying, 'Master, you delivered to me two talents; here, I have made two talents more.'²³ His master said to him, 'Well done, good and faithful servant. You have been faithful over a little; I will set you over much. Enter into the joy of your master.' ²⁴ He also who had received the one talent came forward, saying, '<u>Master, I knew you to be a hard man, reaping where you did not sow, and gathering where you scattered no seed,</u> ²⁵ **so I was afraid, and I went and hid your talent in the ground**. Here, you have what is yours.'²⁶ But his master answered him, 'You wicked and slothful servant! You knew that I reap where I have not sown and gather where I scattered no seed? ²⁷ Then you ought to have invested my money with the bankers, and at my coming I should have received what was my own with interest. ²⁸ So take the talent from him and give it to him who has the ten talents. ²⁹ For to everyone who has will more be given, and he will have an abundance. But from the one who has not, even what he has will be taken away.

When you get into the game, I prophesy that God will allow you to redefine the rules when you partner with His assignment:

1) Talents were given according to each servants' ability

    I prophesy….your Talents will no longer be buried in the ground, due to fear, rejection, misunderstanding or lack of knowledge; YOU WILL CONQUER THIS MOUNTAIN AND FLOW IN THE THINGS THAT GOD HAS

CREATED YOU TO DO FOR HIS WILL TO BE PERFORMED IN THE EARTH!

2) Talents could be used in exchange for more Talents or Money

    I prophesy…..P.O.W.E.R. to Get Wealth! (Provision – Opportunities – Wisdom – Experience – Resilience) Whether you are resilient with one gift or multiple gifts, your focus on maximizing the potential that God has given YOU is going to WORK!

3) Talents that were used in partnership with God's agenda produced exponential return!

    I prophesy…..Now is the time to prepare yourself for double, triple and one-hundred fold returns that are going to overtake you for obedience to God's plan for your life!

A. What should you do with your Talents?

As you read this material, God is shifting your mindset from systematic to strategic! You must develop comfort in change. No longer will you be doing things by habit versus doing things with intention, THERE IS A DIFFERENCE! Doing by way of habit allows you to develop systematic muscles that are the primary defense of an enemy that wants you to be poor and never maximize your potential to be a kingdom financier. Doing with the intention of a strategic outcome aligns your activity to God's will with the expectation that there shall be performance! One of my mentors would ask three (3) requirements of a partner that joins his ministry that was essential to walking in covenant with the ministry and fostering a relationship of continued success: they include, are you willing to share of your Tithe, your Talent and your Treasure? In this instance, we'll just focus on Treasure. As you have worked through the previous chapters in this book and understand the importance of stewardship, we should share a common interest in knowing what to do with the tithe. But what do we do with the things we love most? Let's examine the significance of our talents and treasure that are divinely given by God. It's up to us to use them to manifest destiny in our lives and in the lives of others! So ask yourself as you continue in your journey to achieve milestones of wealth and wellness:

A. What will it cost you to invest in the advancement of your assignment & delegated responsibility?

B. What will it cost others if you do not manifest your assignment to produce a return in the earth? Your ability to produce or inability for that matter is impacting someone, somewhere, right now!

C. Who told you that you could not reap where you did not sow? (In other words, start with the provision or skills that God has given you. Don't ask questions about why you don't have this or that....what have you done already with this or that, which is already in your possession?)

Strategic thinking catapults you into becoming your own Personal Financial Manager or at least acquires the tools to have an educated conversation with those who have been assigned to lead you in the area of your personal finances. **YOU MUST HAVE A TARGET FOR WHERE YOU WANT TO GO!** Get out there and gain some experiences in your profession and in your passion that will essentially propel you into a place of PROMINENCE! Many of us have been poor for years and had self-deprecating mindsets that didn't do anything to move us from the back to the front of the line! This must not be so…..DECLARE & DECREE a thing and it shall be established (Job 22:28)

Repeat these Statements Out Loud:

1) BECAUSE I DESERVE GOD'S BEST, THINGS ARE GOING TO HAPPEN SO FAST MY HEAD WILL SWIM…..

2) BECAUSE I AM THE GAME CHANGER THAT GOD HAS CALLED FROM THE PIT TO THE PALACE, WHATEVER MY HANDS TOUCH WILL PROSPER!

3) BECAUSE GOD HAS FAVORED MY RIGHTEOUS CAUSE IN THE MARKETPLACE, I WILL ASCEND TO THE HIGHEST LEVELS OF GIFTING, GRACE AND GRIT to ACCOMPLISH THE TASK OF MAXIMIZING MY MONEY AND MAGNIFYING MY GOD IN ALL THAT I DO!

Some of us still have low-level thinking because we are comparing ourselves to people who share similar experience and education in their respective fields of interest and are scared to compete for the promises of God as it concerns their career. Some people spend 20 years of more in career positions and never stop to ask others in higher positions of interest how they aspired to achieve the position or consider their own progressive plan for P.O.W.E.R. to Get Wealth!

Declare in your workplace, I'M FOCUSED FOR MY FAITH, I'M FOCUSED FOR MY FAVOR, I'M FOCUSED FOR MY FUTURE!

Roots of Rejection

Roots of Rejection play a role in an impoverished mindset and encourage us to stay on the sidelines as opposed to *Getting in the Game*! Many African-Americans experience symptoms of rejection through broken relationships, inferiority complexes and low self-esteem that have lingered through generations of self-deprecating thoughts of worthlessness embedded during chattel slavery and reinforced through years of Jim Crow, segregation and race inequalities in the United States (abandonment from parents, colorism, etc.). These roots of rejection have been a major contributing factor of minority overspending and financial mismanagement through purchases of high-end luxury items amidst a lack of financial planning as a coping mechanism. In his book entitled, Brainwashed: Challenging the Myth of Black Inferiority, Tom Burrell states "for many of us, life is, and has always been, considered fragile and unpredictable. Since tomorrow is never promised, we must have desired products now – at any and all cost." He went on to state that this attitude explains why our community hesitates to risk our hard-earned money in financial institutions or the stock market. To understand the ABC's of economics in the African American community, we must address our consumer and saving patterns and how they relate to our psychological need to salve 400-year old wounds.

A. Poverty is a mindset!

Until we understand that this is not a concept of rich vs. poor or low income vs. high-wage earners, we will never grasp why some of our best athletes, entertainers and business owners, end up back where they started, building again from the ground up!

B. Can we stop 'putting-on', and actually get-on!

Fake it until you make it is for the birds....the African-American community has over a trillion dollars of exposable income in its reach and needs to leverage those opportunities to break cycles and current trends of poverty and establish decorum for how we will move forward as a community!

C. What's up with all of this debt & spending?

Why are designer labels and expensive cars pimping out our sons & daughters as a pseudo-salve that promotes some sense of value or self-worth based upon a counterfeit image of success and sustainability?

Break all Generational curses in your life!

Preparation for Life's Obstacles

• **D**istractions of Materialism (Haggai 1 / Acts 5)
• **D**angers of Division (Neh. 1-5)
• **D**ilemmas of Hopelessness
   (Prov. 13:12; 15:22)

A. Distractions of Materialism (Haggai 1 / Acts 5)

Because *Intellectual Capital* is a catalyst of change in shifting from financial instability/poverty into financial independence, we must gain confidence & control over the **Seas "C's" of Consumption**:

1) Credit

2) Cribs

3) Cars

4) Clothes

Many minorities in the United States have been distracted by the lure of materialism, attaching feelings of accomplishment and success based upon the cars they drive, houses they inhabit, clothes they wear or by the amassing mounds of debt they can incur due to their ability to be "approved" and swipe credit cards. This false sense of achievement was birthed out of the seed of rejection that began over 400 years ago in chattel slavery. I know, you're thinking what does slavery have to do with my finances or lack thereof? Could it be that your attraction to high-end labels and the continuous sensation to be recognized by your peers based upon what you wear, drive or how you're perceived by others has some correlation to long-term neglect, unresolved hurt or issues that continue to fester and brew due to lack of resolution? **Many of you have a hole in your pocket, because of a dime!** Your inability to see past yourself and understand that God's blessing plan always included community is hindering your progression toward prosperity! (Haggai 1:2-10) **Your seed doesn't have influence or impact because when God gave it to you, it has become consumed by debt, carelessness and over-consumption!** No wonder some of you are sowing in the body of Christ amiss, thinking that your seed is going to put a halt to the bad habits you have walked in for years. Repent, you need to find yourself trying to dig out from the mess you're in before you think that your limited source of revenue has the potential to reach the places God has purposed for it to go! God is the ultimate source who when partnering with his kingdom agenda has the potential to go before us and outpace anything we can do for generations to come!

Over-consumption tends to have us seemingly forget! These actions vehemently contradict the promise in Deuteronomy 8, where God promises to bless us if we continue to REMEMBER HIM! So we find ourselves over-consuming on the account of trying to impress or demonstrate images of success while in reality you have not begun to experience and celebrate the small steps of progression that is your present reality! The reason why some of us can't **Get in the Game** is because your resources are on your back, in your driveway, or squandered on that last vacation you couldn't afford or Christmas gifts that took you way over-budget! Dr. Naim Akbar, author of *Breaking the Psychological Chains of Slavery*, suggested that many African-American Christians associate high-spending on clothing or items that supposedly have significance in putting your best foot forward. Akbar suggested, the major thinkers and scholars (potentially our most powerful agents of change) in African-American communities are often neutralized by a pittance of material goods. This socially destructive phenomenon has its roots deep in the slavery experience. Too often the leaders in our communities have equated a small trinket of material gain with "having arrived." (Akbar, 8)

Dilemmas of Hopelessness / Nihilism (Prov. 13:12, 15:22)

Finance invokes **EMOTIONAL** triggers! In *Race Matters,* Dr. Cornel West suggests some alarming thoughts about nihilism and its generational implications of cultural genocide if not handled in its proper perspectives. There is a sense of worthlessness to those who have been impoverished to the extent that they give up all together. Why do we always have to wait? When will it be our turn? If not today, what prompts you to maintain hope for tomorrow? Well the Bible declares in Proverbs 13:12 NIV, that hope deferred makes the heart sick, but a longing fulfilled is a tree of life. Simply put, a long history of neglect, misfortune, mismanaged and lack of lucrative wage-earning opportunities to provide for your family can cause anyone to go insane! Ask anyone who happened to survive the Great Depression! Even the Centers for Disease Control and Prevention found that overall suicide rates rose and fell with the state of the economy – dating all the way back to the Great Depression. God has a plan for even the foolish things of this world that have hijacked the communities of Black America to a state of self-worthlessness and dejection that has filled our minds with unfruitful behavior! **7P's – "Plans for Progression Prevent the Possibility of Pain from Postponed Promises!"** We must begin to address issues at hand in order to be successful in navigating the game of life. Our ancestral DNA is geared toward confronting acts of injustice and intolerance that plague our ability to grow and achieve, (i.e. slavery revolt, Jim Crow, Mass Incarceration, etc..) so why do we settle in areas of finance and not assemble ourselves to be informed and educated in areas that will create financial independence in our families and communities for generations to come? Instead we allow the emotional rollercoasters of lack of knowledge, bad habits, generational trends etc....to fast track us into lifestyles of poor financial management, poverty and a broken sense of self-love.

Why are we not aware of the major financial hurdles that hinder our community? (i.e. lack of insurance, medical coverage, high/debt spending, and excessive purchase of high-ticket luxury items - cars, clothes, cribs)

Getting in the Game is a clarion call to break the cycle of financial mismanagement and misguided opportunities in your personal life and in your family that impede our community as a whole!

Dangers of Division (Nehemiah 1-5)

Every attempt by the African-American to build a cohesive unit or area for targeting progressive growth in career, finance and educational empowerment has been thwarted by division! In the same circumstance, we see that Nehemiah was presented with the task of rebuilding a community destitute for change. Their collective response to rebuilding God's temple, the place of rejuvenation for the community, was confronted with chaos within its government, opposition to collective bargaining and spending for united purposes, property and ownership rights and impoverished and destitute thinking for resolving its financial woes and political issues. In order to not become a lone soldier as it relates to your pursuing a lifestyle of wealth and wellness, you must assemble other players in the game who are equally excited and motivated about your success, understanding a win for you, is a win for your family, your church and an entire community!

Who's on your team?

- ✓ Professional Coach (Advisor, CPA, Attorney, etc...)

- ✓ Prophetic Coach (Pastor, Spiritual Advisor)

- ✓ Personal Coach (Friend, Mentor)

CHAPTER 8

Get in the Game, pt. II:
EXTRACT!!

───────◆═══◆═══◆───────

Every assignment that has been placed upon your shoulders was done to bring about good! Many of us have experiences, good and bad, in our places of employment and the career path that has been our journey for years that highlight moments of greatness, weakness and opportunities of P.O.W.E.R. to Get Wealth!

We must be able to strategically assess our current situations to resolve all of the unanswered questions that we ponder daily: God when is my time going to come? How do I get to the next level? I'm really good at this…..why am I still not making the money I should be able to attract with these particular skillsets? I want to do more for my family….how? I want to do more for my church….when? I want to do more in my community….with what resources? When we talk about P.O.W.E.R. to Get Wealth, we must understand that embarking upon your journey of building wealth and wellness involves two simple tasks that must be mastered: maximizing income and minimizing taxes. We will focus on maximizing your income in this chapter.

One of the major obstacles that many successful people experience in their professions involves deciding when to sit still versus moving forward. Do I continue to strive for higher paying roles and success within my place of employment or industry, or do I use the skillsets to start my own business?

Many of the skillsets you have built with years of experience in your field of expertise will be the catalyst of change for the WEALTH & WISDOM that God is about to transition you into! Your EXPERIENCE is going to unlock P.O.W.E.R. to Get Wealth! Your EXPERIENCE will be the key factor that closes the deal! Your EXPERIENCE will be the difference to your exploring new contracts, new ideas and new business ventures! The goal is to strategically follow God's plan to establish your leverage that will give birth to strategic advantage in the marketplace! Strategic leverage is causing you to change positions. It's the act of redesigning or rebranding your presence with purpose and intention to be positioned to experience God's grace upon your business or the area of expertise that God has given you to make provision for your family!

You can't win if you don't take the time to develop strategy! You can't win if you never seem to find the time to invest in yourself as much as you invest in others!

God spoke to me several years ago and told me repeatedly in times of prayer and consecration – EXTRACT! One word. Many times I would go back to the Lord in prayer because I didn't understand nor did I have any idea of what was to be applied to the word or situation.

Extract, in the Cambridge English dictionary, means to remove or take out something; especially, to make someone give you something when they do not want to.

I didn't know at the time, the command to **EXTRACT**, was not just for me. It was also for everyone that would read this material and apply strategic principles to current situations that will turn their PAIN into PROGRESSION, their PURPOSE into PASSION, and their PERFORMANCE into PROMISE!

Even as I write, I heard the Holy Spirit say, your <u>vital resources</u> are going to feed you, clothe you, carry you, and comfort you for the rest of your life…..and those with a strategic plan will use the wisdom of the tool to grace generations (their seed) with P.O.W.E.R. to Get Wealth!

Extracting involves your pursuit of progression within your field of expertise by any means necessary. This is not for the faint of heart neither coward soldiers. You must be intentional in your career about where you want to go, the path it takes to achieve your success and holding all parties accountable for their contributions or distractions to your achieving milestones in wealth and wellness. One of the most valuable lessons I've learned in experiencing many bumps and bruises in building a career within financial services is that no matter what role, title or position that I hold, I am ultimately responsible for ensuring my path is aligned to what God has already promised me! I refuse to allow any employer, manager, supervisor or any other person dictate anything contrary to this notion. The conversation was between me and my God, who is Jehovah Jireh, the God who provides more than enough and all other opinions are secondary. I say this with upmost humility because for so long, I was railroaded into positions that did not allow me to maximize my potential skillsets and passion and decided one day that as I continue to craft my passion, I would align my work experiences with my long term goals. Anything that does not support or strategically fit into my long term goals is not allowed to stay. I started my career in a support role but understood that my attention to detail and being resourceful as an expert in my field has allowed me to garner the success that will not be held captive to limited potential or parameters that others have set for me.

I sought God for the path and purpose that he had ordained for me to follow and walked with boldness as I dealt with employers who may not fully understand that I had my own vision for acceleration within my career and they can either participate in that vision or I can find the right environment that highlights my unique difference for promotion. If you're going to walk into your next level of wealth and wellness, you have to trust God to take over the driver's seat in regard to who decides your worth and how the potential that God has given you is maximized and leveraged! Every company you interview with is not the solution to your gifts being maximized and your purpose being leveraged to a place of marketability for next level. It's okay. You have a choice in who takes this journey with you. Settling to accommodate people or firms who don't value your unique difference is never acceptable. However, we understand that while all may not have full understanding of your potential, there are several who are willing to invest in your talent and you must take the opportunity to sharpen your skillsets for growth and greater opportunities down the road.

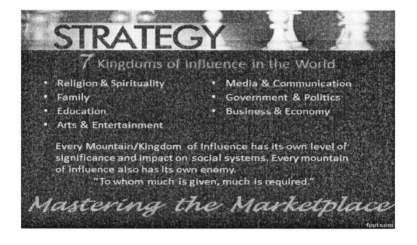

If you desire to excel in your place of employment or explore the possibility of leveraging the skillsets you have developed in a lengthy career to maximize your P.O.W.E.R. to Get Wealth, then you will need to accept the fact that sitting in a position for 20 years waiting on someone to recognize your special talents or UNIQUE DIFFERENCE is not going to happen! There's a saying, good things happen to those who wait. Well, better things happen to those who go

GET IT according to the will of God that has been spoken over their life. The bible encourages us that the kingdom of heaven suffereth violence, but the violent take it by force! There are many things in life that will never become a reality if we remain passive waiting on God to deliver it into our laps. Our faith, without works is dead! Exercising P.O.W.E.R. to Get Wealth is recognizing that we must personally become accountable to being co-laborers of the great gift that God has placed in our hands as stewards of the promise!

Over the span of my almost 20 years of service in financial services, I've been blessed to work in private wealth management with other investment professionals who excel in their field of expertise which has allowed me to build experience in working with investors whose net worth are in the millions. In my normal inquisitive mind, I would always go to God in prayer and ask why would he allow me to work with all of these millionaires and understand their habits that position them for building greater wealth, and not be afforded the opportunity to put these things in practice for myself. It was then that I learned I had been in training for all of these years. What happens if you begin to incorporate strategies at your current financial level that have been used by the wealthy to sustain millions? I would think that change or at the very least, gradual progression toward achieving a lifestyle of wealth and wellness is inevitable!

For every millionaire that I've encountered in my experiences of employment, I've never encountered one who didn't have strategy in place to enhance their plans of action to grow their personal wealth! In order to extract vital resources that propel you into your next level of wealth and wellness, you must **Get in the Game!** Your journey toward achieving milestones in wealth and wellness must be intentional!

Strategic thinkers are who God is looking to advance in the kingdom in order that his word is fulfilled in the earth. These types of people impact culture and trains of thought through their actions. Let's take a look at the fundamentals of strategic planning and its components that will drive your passion and purpose to generate higher levels of income as you maximize your P.O.W.E.R. to Get Wealth!

STRATEGY a plan of action or policy designed to achieve a major or overall aim.

1. **STRATEGIC LEVERAGE** is defined as a company's maneuver (its ability to change its competitive position). Strategic Leverage is achieved as you build & sharpen skillsets that open doors for greater opportunity. Being the best at what YOU do, have its rewards!

2. **STRATEGIC ADVANTAGE** occurs when an individual or entity has a particular characteristic or way of doing things that makes it more successful than others. Strategic Advantage is enhanced through experience.

3. STRATEGIC LOCATION

When you receive a **DIVINE INSTRUCTION**, you are often sent to a **SPECIFIC PLACE**

Everything you want is **SOMEWHERE.**

You belong somewhere.

You do not belong everywhere.

You will succeed somewhere.

You will not succeed everywhere.

When you have identified your strategic location, your gifts will **FLOURISH.**

Am I strategically located in the place God desires for me to be so that he can pour out his blessing plan upon my life?

There is a territory that has your name on it!

**Summary on Strategic Location gathered from Mike Murdock Wisdom Keys teaching on the Law of Place. **

4. STRATEGIC ACCELERATION

"If you don't know where your METRON is being accelerated, you will always be **COMMANDED**   but not **COMMANDING!**

If you don't tell them, they'll tell YOU! (Meaning your potential or place of purpose is not found in others opinions, it's found in God's presence, and the clearer your instructions, the easier you will be able to navigate places that you are supposed to command!)

Your difference creates your rewards!

This is the place where your gifts are being pushed and promoted.

If you do not know your distinctive difference, you will never discern what others need from you.

God placed a part of Himself in you that nobody else possesses. That is what has kept Him protecting you and preserving you.

Am I connected or plugged into a network where I am celebrated and not tolerated?

5. STRATEGIC MOTIVATION

Mistakes or Mentors? There are only two ways to learn….personal experience or personal mentors. Recognizing what you don't have that is COSTING YOU!

Who's on your team?

- **PROFESSIONAL COACH**

- **PROPHETIC COACH**

- **PERSONAL COACH**

Everyone is not called to mentor or download into your spirit, your profession nor your personal life.

Do your mentors reflect the next level you desire to pursue?

Am I strategically aligned with mentors & coaches that help me to achieve my next level?

6. STRATEGIC EXPERIMENTATION

You must make tough decisions and take on roles that will ultimately define and highlight your distinctive difference.

a. Executive level positions (Restructure & Reform)

b. Service level positions (1st Line of Defense, "…….." birthed on the battlefield)

Identify the skillsets that need to be developed!

Make every moment count along the way….establish your **Networks & Net worth!**

Remember, Conversations are birthed out of a place called familiarity!

STOP having conversations with people who don't believe in your dreams! Make QUALITY CONNECTIONS!!! (IF YOU DON'T BELIEVE WHAT GOD IS ABOUT TO DO FOR ME----SUITE YOURSELF!)

Am I taking advantage of opportunities in my sphere of influence that are strategically transitioning me into greater?

7. STRATEGIC IMPLEMENTATION

"…And from the days of John the Baptist until now, the kingdom of Heaven suffereth violence, and the violent take it by force!" – Matthew 11:12

Knowing when to go or forego…..

a. Time to Reclaim

Repairs & Reproduction take place in this stage of implementation. In order to grow your wealth, experience and impact in your field of expertise, your job will be to understand:

HOW DO I REPRODUCE MY STRATEGIC DIFFERENCE IN THE EARTH? This is the stage where you begin to develop and enhance your entrepreneurial skillsets that will allow you to make **Passive Income** (define) in the long term!

b. Time to Retreat

This concept is very important to both the employee and business owner. It is easy to become stale in your course of performing day-to-day activities that do not enhance your natural skillsets and ability that highlight your strategic difference and value! You must decide when it's the right time to abort and abate. Some employees stay in a firm or area of skill too long and never get into the things that God created them to do. This must not be so…..you must walk and move in your purpose or you will always find yourself trying to catch up to your peers that are well on their way in living on purpose and achieving milestones of wealth & wellness! Even for business owners, it could be reinventing a brand or marketing new ideas that will refresh the mission & vision of your organization and essentially breathe new life into it!

c. Time to Release

This concept allows you to reflect on the level of influence you've had in a role/position or your business objectives and decide how to pass it on to others for continued success and implementation. This is the time to also ask yourself the following questions:

1. What have you built?

2. Who have you influenced?

3. How have you used your platform to pave the way for others who share your passion?

Remember people with **P.O.O.R.** mentalities don't discern the seasons & times they are in to execute strategy effectively! **P.O.O.R.** – Pass Over Opportunities Repeatedly

CHAPTER 9

Black Wall Street

Reclaiming our Time: Past, Present and Future!

"Reclaiming my time", is the celebrated slogan crafted by Maxine Waters, U.S. Representative for California, who has over 40 years of public service to the people, the Democratic Party and the United States Congress. Her statement was indicative of a conversation with the Treasury Secretary, regarding financial impropriety between foreign banks and the administration. Her statement was a declaration of bringing order to a somewhat chaotic exchange in dialogue where the house rules were disregarded. In the wake of a conversation that seemed to go way off focus, Ms. Waters was determined to refocus the exchange between her and the Treasury Secretary, in stating "I'm Reclaiming My Time". In *The Hidden Cost of Being African American: How Wealth Perpetuates Inequality*, Thomas Shapiro reminds us that the genius of the American dream is the promise that those who work equally hard will reap roughly equal rewards, be it in wealth, lifestyle, or status.

He suggests that the dialogue on racial inequality often becomes a contentious debate about how level the playing field is, past injustice, and if or how the past affects the present. His arguments conclude that even black and white families with equal accomplishments are separated by a dramatic wealth gap that is widening. Proverbs 6:9 reminds us "now is the time to awake out of our slumber and our sleep". We must ask ourselves the question, "Am I strategically positioned to reclaim my time, celebrate my past, and build legacy for future generations who are the extension of our covenant with God, our families and our communities?" Harboring ill will or holding onto hatred of any kind because of the dark past of our ancestors who suffered because of racial hatred and bigotry, only dampens the opportunity of passing healthy and productive inheritances to millennials and future generations that entrepreneurship, great endeavors and the will of good men has always been the order of our house!

As stewards of God's promises regarding our finances and cultivators of generational wealth for our family and community, we must be tuned in to the pulse of financial obstacles that can deter us from building wealth. Factions and fractions that have historically been the backdrop of communal genocide, race riots and the like are only an indication of the threats that were perceived from onlookers of minority communities who did not understand that we too have great contributions that can be made to our society and strengthen the scope of capitalism and opportunities that should be afforded to everyone.

Black Wall Street was the backdrop and setting of one of the most prominent concentrations of African-American businesses in the United States during the early 20th century. The Greenwood community of Tulsa, Oklahoma, tragically was also the site of one of the bloodiest and most horrendous race riots that the United States had ever seen. It's been ninety-seven years since the race riot of 1921 tore apart a community on the premise of an accusation that incriminated a young black man for the assault of a young white woman. Still to this day, there is no report that shows there was a legitimate conviction of the gentleman or that any crime actually took place. However, the stage had been set for a smokescreen! A smokescreen is defined as a ruse designed to disguise someone's real intentions or activities.

SMOKESCREENS

- Internal and external factors that have the ability to distort what we hear, see or think as it relates to progression, purpose and wealth creation! (We allow distractions to come in and mask themselves with an exterior and a political stunt or front that never belonged to the original storyline!

- There is a "Story within the story"

- Economic Inequalities, Sustainability and distractions…..

- Danger of Divisions & Distractions!!!

- These things are an enemy of cultural dynamics that promote empowerment, sustainability & economic advancement…..

- Distractions of yesterday vs. distractions of today! So the new game of today may not be so much the racial indiscretions of yesterday, but the residue of its pain leaves a wake of destruction and behavioral mismanagement that hinders the African-American community from waking up to take responsibility for social change, progression, policy and performance that will build generational P.O.W.E.R. to Get Wealth!

Out of respect for the descendants of this community and their ancestors who lost their lives on those tragic dates of May 31ˢᵗ and June 1ˢᵗ, I dare not nullify the impact of the loss of this community and the backdrop of racial bigotry and segregation, however, I do wish to highlight the successes of this community that I believe were also key indicators to the reasoning behind their ultimate demise. Black Wall Street, as it was popularly called and the Greenwood community of Tulsa, Oklahoma were thriving and well beyond their time as innovators, business owners and entrepreneurs. This community created opportunities for themselves and created a cultural center that included banks, hotels, cafes, clothiers, theatres, and contemporary homes. Greenwood residents enjoyed many luxuries that their white neighbors did not, including indoor plumbing and a remarkable school system that superiorly educated black children (Josie Pickens, article on The Destruction of Black Wall Street – May 31st, 2013—Ebony.com). This was a community that was strong economically and independent from its surrounding neighbors. Jealousy and or lack of understanding of others and their unique difference opened the door for social evil to be instigated/perpetuated against the black community…..we wrestle not against, flesh and blood, but principalities and powers, rulers of the darkness of this world….spiritual wickedness in high places! The attacks were not just an attack on a people because of race! It was also an attack released against our resources! Resources empower a community to implement and manifest change for a better tomorrow – education, development, invention, mobility, connectivity, etc….Racial Bigotry unleashed social evils in the earth as a smokescreen to imprison people of color to a lifeless sentence of poverty and lack of resources when God ordained us to inherit the earth! The reason some of our children and grand-children will never be exposed to many of the significant achievements and contributions made by African-Americans to our society is because we don't have resources working to influence the decision-makers, or the ability to make the decisions ourselves! Financial independence is a strong indicator of the power and progression of a people. Remember P.O.W.E.R. to Get Wealth is the result of organized people and organized money that are strategically aligned, for the good of the house! And so for some of us, who still think these new opportunities and access to wealth are about a new pair of Gucci shoes, an expensive handbag or a new Mercedes Benz have relegated our community to a sense of impaired judgment and lack of responsibility that hinders the growth and progression of an entire people! I'm not coming against your gadgets. Just make sure they don't get in the way of the real vision.

All hands on deck!

I need your senses to come alive!

I need your access to wealth to facilitate generational change!

Arise from your sleep! Reclaim your time!

Thomas Shapiro, a professor of Sociology and Public Policy at Brandeis University is the author of The Hidden Cost of Being African American and the co-author of Black Wealth/White Wealth. His primary areas of focus are on racial inequality that is perpetuated through wealth. In his research and policy briefs published through the Institute on Assets and Social Policy, he suggested there are several key drivers of the growing racial wealth gap:

- Years of homeownership

- Household Income

- Unemployment (which is much more prominent among African-American Families)

- College Education

- Inheritance (financial support by family, friends and preexisting family wealth)

When reviewing the key drivers that Shapiro suggests are indicators of a growing racial wealth gap, the African-American community needs to acknowledge the misfortunes of our community due to racial bias and injustices that impeded the possibility of successive wealth exchange between generations and use those experiences as a measuring rod to institute policies and progression tactics that will level the playing field. This is not a crisis campaign for sympathy, nor does it condone the deliberate omission of material facts in many of our school systems' history books that forget to tell our story, but it builds the foundation of a conversation that needs to begin in our own households and our own communities that surpass the fulfillment of education goals or even religious experiments that yield to the promise of P.O.W.E.R. that comes from on high. We now have to be bold and daring enough to raise the bar of our desires to incorporate faith that moves, is continuous and an extension of our faith in God! **In order to develop legacy and successive action plans for success, African-Americans in their quest to build sustainable generational wealth must consider the following:**

Learning Task #1: Favor Isn't Fair

Inheritance is the substance of receiving something that is actually apart of one's DNA. You don't have to do anything to acquire an inheritance but continue in the grace and extension of who you were born and created to be. The hardest part of having to rebuild over and over is the thought that somewhere between the lines, some portion of history and integrate details are being lost. One of the things that many African-Americans need to take time to do, if they have not already, is take inventory of the career aspirations and businesses that have been built before them within their own family lineage or area of expertise. Then, ask yourself the questions, do I seem to have similar character traits that will embellish any previous work that was done before me or do I have aspirations that chart new territory within my family? Generally speaking, one of the things that you can do to assess your skill sets and make sure they are leveraging them in the best way could be taking a skills assessment test that can help you identify your natural, God-given abilities to maximize the potential of your skills when implemented in productive environments conducive to your style of learning. One of the skills assessment tests that I took years ago was the Briggs-Myers Test. The results were mind-blowing and allowed me the opportunity to highlight skills that I was under-utilizing in my daily functions and pursuit of my wealth and wellness goals.

Learning Task #2: Leaving an Inheritance

- Insurance – Term policies first. All others are secondary options. Term policies are the most affordable ways of extending your legacy and passing the baton of good stewardship to those who are next in line to inherit the blessings of your hard work. One of the difficult aspects of rebuilding after the destruction and aftermath of Black Wall Street was recovery and implementation of funds back into our communities so that they have the opportunity to thrive again. Many of the residents of Greenwood rebuilt after Black Wall Street, but things changed with desegregation. Given the opportunity to spend money in neighborhoods African-Americans couldn't previously access, many spent elsewhere and eventually moved out of Greenwood, taking business with them. Black Wall Street never re-emerged in Tulsa, but its promise lives on. (www.complex.com/life/2016/09/rebuilding-black-wall-street)

- Estate planning

For those of us who are in the space of growing your wealth well beyond any amount of money that you may have inherited and are in position to pass along the baton of stewardship to loved ones who need the head start in life that you have provided, taking the time to complete an estate plan will allow you to leave instructions regarding your estate. Estate planning allows you the opportunity to lay out the details of who will be responsible to execute the plans of your estate and what to do with the assets that you have accumulated during your lifetime. This allows you to setup entities that may continue to execute your vision long after you are gone as well empower individuals who carry the baton of stewardship that you want to push further in their endeavors.

-   Education planning – Parents don't allow your children to have to tackle the responsibility and burden of how they will educate themselves alone. Some parents get fixated on the fact of their child reaching the age of 18 and decide that they no longer have to participate in the well-being of that child or think all of the responsibility should lie upon their shoulders because they are not adult age. That is so far from the truth. These kids need guidance as they begin to take their first steps into the real world, either going directly into the workforce or to college to better themselves with further education. Prepare for that journey with them! What education savings plans have you setup for them? What career counselors have you spent time with so they are not fumbling through their first few years of college still unsure of their purpose or passions that should be pursued?

Learning Task #3: Passing the Baton of Stewardship

-   Passing the Baton of stewardship is not just a matter of praise and worship. We must pass on godly principles but it must also include financial principles. Avoidance of conversations regarding financial topics and the impact it has had in your life, and in the life of family members needs to be communicated, both good and bad.

-   What does tithe & offering mean to us? Has it allowed us opportunities to seek out better means of living as well business opportunities that may have never been possible? Being able to communicate the impact of great stewardship in your life can have a profound impact on others. Remember, we overcome through the blood of the lamb and the words of our testimonies! (Revelation 12:11)

-   How do we stay connected to God's plan for our finances but incorporate essential money principles that will accelerate our efforts?

Learning Task #4: Mentorship Make-over

-   Inspiring our Youth to take positions of Influence

In this growing age of technology, mentoring our youth leaders of tomorrow is essential to the African-American community and its continued growth and sustainability from within its walls. Young leaders can make vital contributions to society at large as key innovators for socio-economic reform that impacts all Americans, not just the few. Our push toward financial independence and economic sustainability must be successive. Distractions of materialism, dangers of division, and dilemmas of hopelessness are no longer acceptable. We must build bridges with individuals, corporations and service organizations that close the gaps. This will essentially stimulate growth from within and allow us to form partnerships with our brothers and sisters within other communities that strengthen the bonds and opportunity for all within the United States. What is the significance of Black Wall Street that took place in Tulsa, Oklahoma? Why is it significant that millennials learn the history of blacks as it relates to finance, entrepreneurship, homeownership and the efforts to strengthen community so that history does not continue to repeat itself? What are millennials doing now that shows potential for the promise and longevity of success in Black America? What can be done better to strengthen business and communal ties for the future?

Why are we so quick to give up on our own community?

What stereotypes need to be destroyed in order to forge forward in our success? How can the church help these causes? How can the church hinder these causes? What is the sentiment toward capitalism in black America? What can we do for ourselves? What should we not allow to be filtered out of government systems that may not have the best interest of cultivating African American culture?

Why is Black Wall Street important to us now? Strengthening the black community in lieu of its trillion dollar spending capacity has the potential to open more doors for us nationally and globally, allowing all Americans to experience the dream of home ownership, financial independence and a host of other milestones in their wealth and wellness pursuits. One of the lessons to learn here is that regardless of scare tactics, hostile takeovers or the onslaught of violence, WE STILL RISE! No man or system has the power or ability to stop or come against what God has already ordained to succeed! Many corporations today are even finding out that diversity is actually a good thing, and a good thing that they must be willing to embrace, or suffer the consequences! The success and sustainability of their corporations are contingent upon the ability to recruit and attract the most talented individuals that can work together while serving blended families, races and communities that are a part of the United States of America. Any injustice that we face, even in today's world could not only be an indication of race or gender bias, but also socio-economic inequality that has continued to esteem other race groups while African-Americans are left holding the bag. Too many times, we have had to start over from scratch, trying to build and pass on an inheritance that has been beaten, broken and battered by outsiders who didn't understand at the time, the unique difference of African-Americans and the contributions they can make to society. In order to achieve and further extend legacies that grow from one generation to another, we must know the history of what has already been accomplished, its setbacks, and what we can learn and enhance from this day forward. Where do we go from here? These race riots and a host of other social injustices toward the African-American community did not just hurt our economic opportunities for sustainability; they also left the weight of low self-esteem, hopelessness and fear of abandonment and rejection within a nation that we helped to build!

RECLAIMING MY TIME....RESILIENCE TO WIN!

The good news is that when we talk about P.O.W.E.R. to Get Wealth, we understand the last component of this life-changing strategy for wealth creation will catapult us into next-level living achieved through the MIND, MONEY and MINISTRY of God's Word to remain RESILIENT in times of opposition. Quitters never win! In the game of life, repetition plus consistency breeds success. From month to month, and year to year, you must declare with confidence, that you will reclaim and redeem your time. Time is a precious commodity and I was frequently told by my mentors that we have more time, than we have money! Most people look at their bank accounts and investments with great detail and assess how much money they have to spend, invest or give away. Coincidentally, many of us never look at time the same way, and mistakenly overlook this valuable resource. Resilience is the capacity to recover quickly from difficulty or toughness, knowing that time is of essence. So why does resilience matter? Resilience, is knowing what God said, even in the face of opposition that wants to write another ending to your story. God is the author (writer, creator, innovative thinker) and finisher of our faith! I love the message Bible version that says,

Do you see what this means – all these pioneers who blazed the way, all these veterans cheering us on? It means we'd better get on with it. Strip down, start running – and never quit! No extra spiritual fat, no parasitic sins. Keep your eyes on Jesus, who both began and finished this race we're in. Study how he did it. Because he never lost sight of where he was headed – that exhilarating finish in and with God – he could put up with anything along the way; cross, shame, whatever. And now he's there, in the place of honor, right alongside God. When you find yourselves flagging in your faith, go over that story again, item by item, that long litany of hostility he plowed through. That will shoot adrenaline into your souls! (Hebrews 12:1-3 MSG)

Resilience is what keeps you when you become overwhelmed with the opposition you face in your workplace or business that you endeavor to build and leave a legacy! Resilience is what carries you when spiritual warfare has been escalated and distractions, disruptions and smokescreens come to shift your focus away from your purpose, your progression and your P.O.W.E.R. to Get Wealth! **Resilience is actually one of the most vital components to P.OW.E.R. because it's the substance that won't allow you to settle into patterns of procrastination, lack of action and complacency that fuels poverty mindsets that have paralyzed our resources!** Resilience is the final ingredient and component of P.O.W.E.R. that was poured out of God's spirit into you that allows you to read this material that will strategically catapult you into next-level living for your family, your church and your community! Societal reformation is possible but it will require a new vision and a new faith coupled with P.O.W.E.R. to Get Wealth that surpasses your traditional church clichés of naming and claiming the promise for your house! Black Wall Street is a reminder to the African-American community to stay alert and maximize every opportunity to excel in your field of expertise knowing there is a generation behind us who cannot afford to start over. **Black Wall Street is a reminder to our community that in spite of opposition and lack of understanding that floods our walls of resistance, our ability to reclaim our time is the testament of our strength as a people and as productive citizens who contribute to the vibrancy and velocity of these United States of America.**

CHAPTER 10

Finance 101

This chapter has been dedicated to uncovering and identifying ways you can move forward out of poverty and into prosperity and experience the God-life that has been promised to all believers who have seed in the ground! If you have additional questions that may not be highlighted in this area, please feel free to send questions to our team at gotquestions@milestoneswealth.org. Our team of Stewardship Coaches will be glad to assist you!

***Disclosure: For your specific situation, please see an investment professional who can review your profile and make specific recommendations in accordance to that investment profile. The information contained in these responses does not constitute an offer of investment advice. Please see an Investment professional prior to making any decisions regarding your portfolio. ***

Stewardship

Does the obligation to tithe still apply to a New Testament Church?

Yes, Yes, Yes!!! I get so tired of believers who want to debate the topic of whether tithing is still relevant because it was talked about more so in Old Testament context. But we're not just a New Testament Church. The bottom line is, shouldn't every believer want to be charitable, especially to those less fortunate as well to the household of God so that the work of ministry can be supported locally and globally to spread the message of the gospel? Well, 2 Corinthians 8:7 (NIV) also says, "But since you excel in everything – in faith, in speech, in knowledge, in complete earnestness and in the love we have kindled in you – see that you also excel in this grace of giving." That being said, 'Getting in the Game' and 'For the Good of the House' also helps you understand that the tax structure of this country rewards those who share.

When is the best time to teach my children about tithing and giving? Once children know the value of money, they should know the value of giving. The bible says, train up a child in the way they should go, when they get older, they won't depart from it. The scripture was built on the premise of discipline. This discipline works in the area of tithing and sowing. It will start with allowance and then evolve into how they discipline themselves with their salaries and paychecks as an adult.

Doesn't God understand that I don't tithe; because I don't agree with what the church does with MY money? No, God does not understand. One of the things that I think every believer should have is a sense of urgency when it comes to supporting the things of God. Understand that the Law of Reciprocity states that what you make happen for God's House, God makes happen for your house! That being said, you don't have to agree with everything the church is doing with the money. Sometimes there are projects going that you are not fully privy to the logistics of what it takes to reach its final destination. However, stay alert and discerning. There are times when there may be cases of abuse by your local church. In those times, I think it's best to find a local worship assembly where you can grow spiritually that happens to meet your guidelines of how the business initiatives of the church are handled and sow your tithe there.

Can I tithe my time rather than my money to the church? No, money is an indicator of your health and habits. However, there are times when tithing or sowing in time does yield dividends that will help you in the long term. Matthew 6:21 says, for where your treasure is, there your heart will be also. Go through your transaction menu or online statement. Highlight or star the recurring items. This quick illustration will quickly identify what you really support. Whether it's eating out, fitness and health, reading or other activities. A good steward should be able to see that they have allocated their resources, not just time, to the house of God, and also to their savings or investment accounts.

Is it ok to give some of my tithe money to family and friends who need financial assistance? No, No, No! Now that you have received the revelation of P.O.W.E.R. to Get Wealth, you understand that it is God's wealth distribution plan for those that sow into God's system first! When you sow into God's system first, he will make provisions to take care of all other things that are dear to your heart, including your family. Matthew 6:33 NLT says, "Seek the kingdom of God above all else, and live righteously, and he will give you everything you need." Stewardship comes into play here as well. Being a good steward is not just about tithe but also the remaining portion of your income that God expects you to use good judgment and Godly wisdom is making decisions about how the rest of the money will be used to advance the kingdom and your personal endeavors. Do you want to spend most of your time paying other people's bills or do you have a system in place that could help them be self-sufficient and lend help on occasion where there are dire needs.

I have my own business. Do I tithe off of gross revenues or personal income? This question can get very technical. When you are talking about personal versus business income, they are very different categories because they each have a list of itemized expenses that may differ greatly. In this case, costs that are associated with having a corporation and all of its expenditures and overhead differ from that of a sole proprietor or solely owned LLC. I think the focus here again is the posture of a good steward. It may be best, as a business owner, to set aside a specific salary that is inclusive of maintaining other reserves that will sustain the business. Addressing the issue of tithing can come out of the personal income that has been reserved as an employee of the business. But keep in mind, there are a number of companies who are good citizens and commit to charitable acts of giving in the name of their organization. It has tax benefits for the company as well help to further the mission of the non-profit organizations who receive their help.

Once I give my tithe to the church, do I have full control over the remaining 90% of my income? Yes, but take caution. Being a good steward is understanding that everything you have is because of the measure of gifts, talents and preferential treatment that God has bestowed upon your life. How you treat your money is an indication of your level of grace and gratitude of God's blessings! Keep in mind that tithe, is the entry level commitment of giving in the Lord's house. The scripture declares in Malachi 3 that a man can rob God in tithe and offerings. Your tithe is a requirement of your trust and commitment to God's plan for your life. Your offerings shed light on your love for God and the blessings in your life. This is the time where you can begin to grow and learn charitable giving, budgeting, spending, saving and self-control.

What should I do with my tithes if I don't have a church home?

Stop what you are doing. LISTEN. This is a pivotal time in your life where the seed you sow can literally make room for your spiritual blessing and the direction of your life to prosper from this moment forward. You may not have a local church. However, using your free time to actively identify a ministry that embodies the same core values and faith principles that you have is essential to your sowing on good ground! Once you have identified that ministry and stand in alignment with its core values, mission and faith principles, you can sow your tithe there, whether you have officially joined the ministry or not. Take note, bringing your tithe into God's storehouse, so there is sufficiency in his house, will allow God to rebuke the devourer so that you will not miss a beat while securing a new church home. It may be the seed and tithe that actually fast-track you to finding destiny in your new church!

If I'm unemployed or in-between jobs am I required to still tithe?

In this example, you may not be able to tithe of your monetary increase to the church, but this is the time when I believe sowing of your time and talent to the ministry of your choice comes into play. The posture of a truly good steward is always GIVING! This may be the time that you think, you don't have anything to give. But fret not, you actually have a lot to give and can use these gifts and your time to still advance the kingdom.

Budgeting & Debt

How often should I go over my budget, spending or savings plan?

In order to achieve a lifestyle of wealth and wellness, you need to review your spending habits at least on a monthly basis. Once you have identified areas where you do well, as well those areas that fall short, you can make necessary adjustments as you go through the following month with the intention to implement these habits for the long haul. One of the best apps I think that tracks your spending habits, allows you to setup alerts when you are nearing the edge of a monthly spending limit, and can auto-sync information into the app once you log into your personal accounts is Mint.com. And better yet, it's FREE! There are other apps out there that do the same thing but have underlying costs associated or you have to manually feed your account information into the application, which can be extremely time consuming.

How much should I save for an emergency expense?

The general rule of thumb regarding emergency savings is 6 months of income. That means whatever it takes to pay all of your bills on-time and still meet normal household requirements (i.e. groceries, gas, rent/mortgage). Take the total expense for one month and multiply times six. I think this number can seem overwhelming especially if you are attempting to climb out of arrears, so a three month target could be good to start with and build out to 6 months over time as you pay down any debt or outstanding items that would prevent you from having an emergency expense.

Who should take the lead on personal finances in the home; husband or wife? The traditional responsibility of leading the household belongs to man. God created the union between man and woman for him to be assisted in this endeavor. However, societal trends show that women who actively work outside of the home also provide great leadership skills and problem solving that are essential to achieving a lifestyle of wealth and wellness. That being said, I believe ALL HANDS should be on deck. As couples tend to share or delegate various responsibilities, you quickly identify those where one spouse may be stronger that the other and vice versa. Leverage your strengths wisely. Husbands don't be prideful if your wife is able to offer a wise solution to your financial problems. You are a team. Make it fun and celebrate your financial independence together!

I don't agree with the way my spouse handles the finances, can't I keep a little money on the side? No, no and NO. Women, I know your mother probably told you to always keep a stash on the side. This traditional mindset breeds contempt and dishonesty. A family should be honest with each other if they are going to achieve success as a family. This cannot be achieved if one spouse is being dishonest in their earnings and how any additional income is being directed. Fellas, if you are married, your income is not your own. Budgeting should identify which items are necessities versus wants and how you will achieve your dreams as a team, as opposed to obtaining them on your own or deceitfully.

Cash / Credit

What is the fastest way to pay off my credit card debt?

One of the fastest ways to pay off your credit card bills is to line them up by interest rates, highest to lowest, considering the size of the balances of those cards that need to be paid off. As you pay off one card, use the minimum that was applied to the former card recently paid off to compound your monthly payment being applied to balances. I think it's also best to keep in mind that if you have cards that have extremely different loan balances, sometimes take one of the smaller ones to pay off quickly, then allocate that monthly fee toward the remaining cards to fast track the payoff. Paying off the smaller cards quickly builds the motivation to stay on track and know that debt freedom is a reality that can be accomplished!

A debt collector has contacted me about an old debt. Do I have to pay it?

It depends. Every state has a statute of limitations which governs how long the creditor or bill collector has to sue you. If the debt is too old, the statute of limitations may protect you where you may not have to repay the item. A good way of being able to tell how old your outstanding item is would be to check the status of it on your credit report. It should show hold old the item is, contact information and what options may be best in order to resolve the outstanding debt. You don't have to run your credit report every time to do this. Simply go online and start an account with www.creditkarma.com or any other agency of your choice that provides free access and review of your credit file. You can even download the app to a mobile device.

Is it necessary to have credit cards?

I personally believe in total debt freedom, but especially freedom of credit card debt. However, I do understand in cases of shortage of income, there may be times when you need to use credit in the short term in order to resolve emergencies. One of the things that you should instead focus on is building your savings and assets. Did you know that having assets even in an investment account can be used as leverage to secure your own line of credit? Many wealthy people do not use traditional lines of credit, such as credit cards, and use their personal wealth as a means of achieving the best rates on loans or use cash to pay for expenses. Besides, it's not the end of the world to not have a credit card, and certainly those who have sufficient cash savings, investments and financial plans in place only use credit cards for reward perks and incentives that are offered in exchange for the money that they spend on a monthly basis anyway. You could use it for monthly spending, staying within your budget, and then pay off the card at the end of each month, using the reward points as a bonus for travel and other savings.

I am paying down my debt. Why is my credit score dropping?

Keep in mind that your FICO score is an indicator of how well you manage debt. So if you happen to be paying down major lines of credit and revolving debt, so that you can live a debt free life, your credit may take a hit. The most important thing is that you are living within your means and you are rewriting the rules to the game. If you are also building wealth at the same time, you are positioning yourself to leverage the assets you have accumulated to secure future lines of credit.

What is the difference between credit counseling vs. filing bankruptcy?

I think one of the major differences between credit counseling and filing bankruptcy is the protection granted to the petitioner under the law. Credit counseling may be a good route when you need a plan and your current position still affords an opportunity of resolution that is within reason. However, if your debt or financial situation is far gone, bankruptcy may be an option that allows you to start over and implement new strategy so that you don't have to face this positioning again! I know as a Christian some of you may shun the idea of bankruptcy and say that it is walking away from your responsibilities to pay and a lack of good stewardship. I agree to some extent. However, not having a good track record of stewardship does not mean that you cannot use the law to accept the reality of the situation and use it as a learning tool for making better decisions in the long-term. The laws of the land afford us the opportunity to receive grace in our time of need and reposition ourselves to prosper according to God's will. As Christians, we should not support an intentional lack of integrity in resolving your debts or obligations to pay, however, there are laws in place to protect our rights as citizens to rebuild and become productive participants in society.

I co-signed an auto loan for my daughter. When I tried to refinance my mortgage, I found out she has been paying it late, and it has hurt my credit score. What can I do to get that information removed? One piece of advice I have for co-signers; DON'T! Most people tend to do this because the person they are attempting to help establish credit is either over-extended with debt or has yet to establish it. In both cases, this proves that their credit-worthiness has either not been revealed, or it has ALREADY BEEN REVEALED, that they are not to be trusted! Remember, Proverbs 22:7 states the borrower is subject to the lender. When you co-sign a loan and the primary borrower fails to make timely payments according to the contractual agreement, your signature states that you will pick up any slack when the borrower falls short. That means congratulations; you're the owner of a new car!

Cribs (Homes & Real Estate)

Help. I am saving my money well and ready to purchase my first home. Where do I begin?

Start with a Pre-Approval. This will help you to find out how much home you can afford! Any lender or mortgage loan provider can let you know what information they require to work up a magic number that lets you know how much house you can afford. After getting that number, I would suggest asking the lender based upon their current rates and your credit file what your mortgage amount would be in you spent the full amount of the approval versus spending an amount that is not at the top of your max limit for approval. The goal as a new home owner who is attempting to build a lifestyle of wealth and wellness is to stay within your budget! Also having a pre-qualified letter lets the seller know that you are a serious contender. Although some can be nice and go along for the ride at times, none of the real estate professionals want to go through a long process with a potential buyer, showing them multiple homes, etc…to only find out that they can't secure financing to close the deal. You want to keep your Real Estate Agent on your good side and know that you are making their job easy….in the end, the good ones will make sure you get a good deal on your purchase! Warning: Keep in mind, you don't have to show the seller your full approval amount, when you are ready to negotiate, you can have your lender produce proof of your pre-approval that matches the negotiated price of the home, so you are not paying more than the negotiated price. This means you do not have to spend the max allowable amount of your pre-approval. Besides, the seller should not know this amount in your negotiations; just know that you have proof of financing when you are ready to head toward the closing table!

What are some of the key things that a first-time homebuyer should be aware of when purchasing? (Home expenses not to exceed 30% of AGI)

A good rule of thumb is to keep your home expenses within the range of 30% of your adjusted gross income. As a first-time homebuyer, you will need to understand that the mortgage payment is not the only expense you will have for the house. You will need to consider all of the "extras" that come along with being a new homeowner. These extras can include lawn maintenance, roof repairs, and unexpected disasters, such as a water heater replacement, and burst pipes. You also have utility bills to consider (water, heat, gas, electric, home protection services, HOA). When all of these line items are considered in your budget you want to make sure you are not spending more than half your income on maintaining a house. The goal here is to enjoy the home, not to be HOUSE POOR. Allow it to be a wealth stream toward building equity and net-worth for securing greater wealth for the long term.

What mortgage term options do I have? Which ones are best if I want to pay off my home faster? What terms are best if I want the lowest payment?

Most traditional mortgage loans are done as 30 year loans. Think about it, for most of us, it's the biggest investment you have made. However, before you make a final decision about the loan term, consider where interest rates currently stand and if selecting a shorter loan term (i.e. 20yr, 15yr, etc.) would be a better option for you. When I originally closed on my first home some years ago, I started off in a 30 year term. A few years had passed and I saw that there was not a significant change in the balance I owed on my home so I began to inquire about current interest rates and to my surprise, was told it was more than 1% lower than the original contract. I was able to find out that changing from a 30yr term to a 15year term would only cause my mortgage to increase by $100 dollars. The moral of the story is, I refinanced my home, with a lower rate, barely changed my mortgage payment and knocked more than 10 years off of the life of my home. It has caused the equity in my home to skyrocket along with increases in home prices in the area coupled with the fact that I am paying down the debt at a much faster rate. Traditional 30 year loans may have a lower payment for a new homeowner, however, if you have been in a home for more than two years and have become accustomed to the costs associated with home ownership, you may want to see where current mortgage rates are and if it's feasible for your to fast-track your path to debt freedom by paying off the home faster in a shorter loan term such as 15yr or 10yr terms.

I purchased a home and over the years it has spiked in value. I am going to sell it and cash out my savings. Is there anything I need to know?

If you qualify for the exclusion, you may do anything you want with the tax-free proceeds from the sale. You are not required to reinvest the money in another house. But, if you do buy another home, you can qualify for the exclusion again when you sell that house. Here's the most important thing you need to know: To qualify for the $250,000/$500,000 home sale exclusion (single vs. married filing jointly), you must own and occupy the home as your principal residence for *at least two years before you sell it.* Your home can be a house, apartment, condominium, stock-cooperative, or mobile home fixed to land.

If you meet all the requirements for the exclusion, you can take the $250,000/$500,000 exclusion any number of times. But you may not use it more than *once every two years.*

The two-year rule is really quite generous, since most people live in their home at least that long before they sell it. (On average, Americans move once every seven years.) By wisely using the exclusion, you can buy and sell many homes over the years and avoid any income taxes on your profits.

Should I get a home inspection?

Once you have put in an offer on a home, you typically need to schedule a home inspection prior to closing. A home inspector will take the time to thoroughly investigate major systems and appliances – the roof, electricity, heating and air, plumbing – to make sure they meet certain guidelines to prevent short-term major expenses that the new purchaser would experience after closing on the home. This will give you an opportunity to address those issues and present them to the seller as conditions to correct prior to the closing date or forfeit the deal.

When can I back out if I change my mind?

Buyers can always back out of a deal, but without contingency loopholes, they may risk losing the earnest money (cash put down to secure the offer, typically around 1-2% of the home's price). Contingencies are the best way to back out of a real estate purchase. Typically unsatisfactory home inspections and subject to appraisal conditions leave the door open if unsatisfying to the buyer as well as the lender of the loan.

Education

I can't afford my student loan payments, what options do I have?

If you are in a position where you have student loans and you cannot afford to pay them, doing nothing is NOT AN OPTION! You can easily lose your home or other assets when you default on student loan payments. There are options to repayment which include deferment, forbearance, income-driven repayment plans, etc....Talk with your loan provider to see what options you can take to secure your future and continue to move toward debt freedom, wealth and wellness.

What should take priority: saving for my retirement or investing in my children's education? This is a hard question to tackle for many people because you think of all the variables in one direction or another; I've lived my life, what about my child, I have a responsibility, etc...The best thing you can do for your children is to be self-sufficient and financially independent, where you don't become a burden even in retirement upon their shoulders with no resources or assets intact. If you can't afford to save additional funds for education planning of your children, provide them at least a stable home environment. This means having insurance coverage, retirement planning, homeownership, etc....if you can't pay their way through college, you can at least provide the tools that steer them in the right direction. Be proactive in researching opportunities for scholarships and grants. Have faith in God; there are more ways than one to skin a cat!

When is the best time to begin saving for my child's education?

As soon as you can get a social security number for them after they're born, use it to open an account to begin saving for their future. Remember, slow and steady will win the race! When you begin investing early, growth in the market along with compound interest will do wonders.

What is a 529 Savings Plan?

A 529 plan is an education savings plan sponsored by a state or state agency. Savings can be used for tuition, books, and other education-related expenses at most accredited two- and four-year colleges and universities, U.S. vocational-technical schools, and eligible foreign institutions. Savings may also be used for tuition expenses at eligible public, private, and religious primary and secondary educational institutions (K-12).

U.S. residents of any state, who are 18 years of age or older (or the age of majority in some states), may invest in most state plans. There are significant tax advantages to using these plans which include earnings growing federal income tax deferred as well eligibility for state tax deductions.

What education savings vehicles are available for me to use for my children? What happens if my child decides not to attend college? The most prevalent education savings vehicles are 529 plans. Review the section questions on this education plan and its functionality. One of the best features of the plan also allows generation skipping if a beneficiary decides against going to college. You can select a family member to gift any balance of the funds you have saved, so taking the option to plan ahead will never be a bad investment.

Retirement Planning

What's the difference between Traditional IRAs vs. Roth IRAs?

Traditional and Roth IRAs differ in regard to three major areas: income limits or income-eligibility rules, tax incentives and withdrawal rules.

Anyone with earned income who is younger than 70½ can contribute to a Traditional IRA. Whether the contribution is tax deductible depends on your income and whether you or your spouse (if you're married) are covered by a retirement plan through your job, such as a 401(k). See IRA deductibility chart.

Roth IRAs don't have age restrictions, but they do have income-eligibility restrictions: Single tax filers, for instance, must have modified adjusted gross incomes of less than $135,000 in 2018) to contribute to a Roth IRA. (Contribution limits are phased out starting with a modified AGI of $118,000—$120,000 in 2018—per IRS guidelines.) Married couples filing jointly must have modified AGIs of less than 199,000 in 2018) in order to contribute to a Roth; contribution limits are phased out starting at $186,000 ($189,000 for 2018).

Both Traditional and Roth IRAs provide generous tax breaks. But it's a matter of timing when you get to claim them. Traditional IRA contributions are tax-deductible on both state and federal tax returns for the year you make the contribution; withdrawals in retirement are taxed at ordinary income tax rates. Roth IRAs provide no tax break for contributions, but earnings and withdrawals are generally tax-free. So with Traditional IRAs, you avoid taxes when you put the money in. With Roth IRAs, you avoid taxes when you take it out in retirement. **Of course, with both types of IRAs, you pay no taxes whatsoever on all of the growth of your contributed funds, as long as they remain in the account.**

Traditional IRAs:

- Contributions to Traditional IRAs generally lower your taxable income in the contribution year. That lowers your adjusted gross income, helping you qualify for other tax incentives you wouldn't otherwise get, such as the child tax credit or the student loan interest deduction. (Note that if you or your spouse has an employer retirement plan, your ability to deduct contributions may be reduced or eliminated.)

- If you are under 59½, you can withdraw up to $10,000 from your account without the normal 10% early-withdrawal penalty to pay for qualified first-time home-buyer expenses and for qualified higher education expenses. Hardships such as disability and certain levels of unreimbursed medical expenses may also be exempt from the penalty; however, you'll still pay taxes on the distribution.

Roth IRAs:

- Roth contributions (but not earnings) can be withdrawn penalty- and tax-free at any time, even before age 59½.

- If you are under 59½, you can withdraw up to $10,000 of Roth earnings penalty-free to pay for qualified first-time home-buyer expenses, provided at least five tax years have passed since your initial contribution

How much should I be saving to a retirement account?

The industry-wide rule of thumb is to target 15% of your disposable income toward savings. It will allow you to save at a pace that will stay ahead of inflation considering compounding interest over time, and allows you to approximate number of periods required for doubling your investment. See Rule of 72. Some employers now attempt to help employees with their retirement savings by auto-enrollment at an entry level on average of 3%. My suggestion to you is to find out what your company match or incentive rate for participation and do at least the minimum to get a full match until you are available to increase your contribution percentage over time. For example, if your company provides a dollar-for-dollar match up to 4 percent, then by deferring/contributing four percent of your earned income, you will have saved eight percent on the year.

What should I do with my retirement savings if I'm leaving my job?

You always have the option to confirm if your savings will be better invested with a Financial Advisor at any investment, brokerage firm or mutual fund company or decide to keep the assets invested within the 401k or retirement savings vehicles at your employer. Typically an investment, brokerage firm or mutual fund company may have a wider selection of investment choices. Cost savings is key here in order to manage or self-direct your investments. Keep in mind that most company plans will not allow you to house them if assets do not exceed $5,000. If you elect to choose an outside financial services provider, you will need to setup a Traditional or Rollover IRA with them and process the move of money from your employer to the service provider as a Direct Rollover. Doing this allows you to avoid an upfront 20% federal tax withholding by not taking ownership of the funds immediately! Who wants to pay taxes on their own money immediately for not following that rule?

Is there a way to catch-up on my retirement savings if I didn't do a good job of saving in my early years? Yes, Congress added the catch-up contribution provision to retirement plans out of concern that baby boomers hadn't been saving enough for retirement. This option enables savers age 50 and over to increase contributions at a time when retirement draws near. Age-50 catch-up contributions are possible in 401k, 403b and 457 plans, and IRAs, but the rules differ among plans. A catch-up contribution is any elective deferral made by an eligible participant that is in excess of the statutory limit ($18,500 in 2018), an employer-imposed plan limit, or any limit applied in order for the plan to satisfy the ADP nondiscrimination test for the year. The maximum amount of catch-up contributions that can be contributed in 2018 is $6,000. Plan participants who are or will turn 50 years of age during the calendar year are eligible to make catch-up contributions. However, the participant's regular plan contributions must reach at least one of the following limits before catch-up contributions can begin: the annual deferral limit, the plan's deferral limit, or the annual ADP limit for Highly Compensated Employees. You also have catch-up contribution provisions for IRAs. Currently the max contribution to an IRA is $5,500. For those IRA owners who attain age 50 during the current calendar year are allowed to add an additional $1,000 for a total of $6,500 total for IRA owners over the age of 50.

What retirement options are available for small-business owners?

If you are a self-employed business owner who is looking for the most cost effective way to lower your taxes and help you save for retirement, then opening a SEP (Simplified Employee Pension) IRA may be a good way to build your retirement nest egg. Most employees are limited to the traditional $18,500 contribution limit for 2018 according to IRS guidelines. For those who are self-employed, that number changes to an allowable contribution of up to $55,000 for 2018 or 25% of your eligible employee compensation, whichever is less. The compensation limit for 2018 is $275,000. Small business owners have a few additional options for retirement savings that include Solo 401k's but the SEP IRA's administrative process for setup and account opening is more streamlined. There are a few requirements to qualify for participation in a SEP IRA. Please see your tax advisor, retirement education professional or an investment specialist for further details. Other benefits to opening a SEP IRA include: (1) accelerating your retirement savings over time, (2) creating a major tax deduction and reduction in your taxable income, and (3) you have the ability to expand your SEP IRA to cover employees.

Investing

How do I begin investing in the stock market?

One of the easiest ways to begin investing in the stock market is through your employer retirement plan accounts (i.e. 401k, Thrift Savings Plan, 403B, etc...). Ariel Investments' study on Black Investors Survey stated that is it the gateway to many minorities entering the stock market. You can earn a company match, essentially free money, as a way of saying thank you for participating in your own savings plan. This allows you to have access to various stocks or mutual funds and other investment choices that may be an underlying asset of a particular investment holding. Use the library of materials that are typically located in your company retirement website for employees to get your feet wet and learning information at your own leisure. Besides, you would have a retirement support desk that you can use to ask any questions regarding those investments and the advantages of using the account. Relax, unwind and enjoy your journey toward creating wealth!

What types of investments are available to the average person?

Stocks are probably the most well-known option, but picking and choosing individual companies to invest in is not how most people get involved in the market. Instead, you may want to consider an index fund, which invests in the securities included in indexes like the S&P 500, Dow Jones or those that track particular sectors. Another option for those who may be limited in the actual start-up amount that they are able to invest would be mutual funds. There are opportunities to purchase funds that already have a wide range of diversification within sectors and holdings in the one fund. Many of them include periodic investment programs (PIP) that allow you to invest on either monthly or quarterly schedules to build your nest egg over time.

Is it risky to pick out your own stocks?

If we were all so lucky to pick our own stocks and have enough success to become millionaires then many of us would not be taking the gruel path of 20-30 years of work and the stress that comes along with it. Studies show that choosing stocks is almost always a losing proposition, even for the pros. In addition, trading stocks actively can get very expensive. Most programs are geared to extend discounts on trades to the active trader, in which many who would take this risk on their own most times will spend way more money than they actually made. Most firms also discount management fees to those investors with larger deposits. Typically those investors who have larger deposits will take the option to have their accounts actively managed by professionals that will setup their portfolios for targeted performance over time. Just ask questions when you need and most advisors will inform you of their fee structures that are associated with investing your assets. There is no need to be scared or fearful, but keep in mind that the stock market is not a place where you want to throw money into random investments where there has not been any research, strategic or logical advice provided that helps you to make an informed decision. Take time to learn by asking questions to an investment professional and you will be good to go!

Why is risk tolerance important, and how can I figure out what mine is?

Risk tolerance measures the level of risk an investor is willing to take in order to build an investment portfolio over a specified period of time. Typically if you select an investment advisor of choice that you will work with, they will provide a questionnaire that typically covers about 8-10 questions that gauge scenarios regarding risk, your level of comfort and the timeframe you are willing to invest savings without withdrawing funds.

Why is diversification important to my investment portfolio?

It is extremely important to diversify assets so that you won't have all of your eggs in one basket. For example, once your risk tolerance rating is identified, your investment advisor may setup a portfolio that has various items – stocks, bonds, cash, etc. – in it. Some may be held to maintain your account growth, while others may be held to grow more aggressively over a period of time. Diversification helps to soften the blow in case of a down market. However, diversification helps to grow the portfolio while some others remain stable or flat, in a growing economy.

Why should I prioritize retirement over non-retirement investing?

Over 35% of people in the United States have less than $1,000 of savings tucked away for retirement. And with modern life span calculations, you could expect to live about 30 years as a retired person. When you think of the expenses that could be incurred in retirement along with healthcare and limited income outside of one's own personal savings, you do the math! One of the best opportunities to grow your wealth, with compounding interest, in a tax-sheltered vehicle is in your retirement savings account. Take advantage of your company's 401k, 403b or various retirement savings plan, most have incentives or matching programs to encourage your savings habits.

How often should I check on the status of my investment portfolio?

A new investor will typically check their portfolio status more often than they should. I get it, you are new to this concept and getting comfortable in understanding that investing in the stock market is for the long haul can be challenging. However, as an investor you need to understand that there will be swings in the market, in both directions, up and down. The savvier investor on average may review the portfolio with an investment advisor 1-2 times annually. As a point of reference, you may want to set a reminder to review it yourself quarterly to see how the performance is doing and if you have any questions, reach out to an investment professional. They will normally be able to answer questions as it relates to trends and its current impact on the markets.

How do I know my advisor will look out for my best interest?

Don't fret my friends, the securities and investment arena has numerous checks and balances to help identify and safeguard clients as it relates to their investment portfolios, their interest and best practices. Keep in mind that all investments have some level of risk, however there are tools to help identify the risk associated with a specific investment choice and your advisor should be able to communicate that level of risk in order for you to make an informed decision. Risk ratings, performance sheets, compliance guidelines and a host of other tools are steadily monitored to help facilitate your investment journey. Of course, there is always a bad apple or two in the bunch. Make sure to review your statements and ask questions if there is something you don't understand or feel comfortable with. Investing is a journey that you should feel good about as it moves you toward a lifestyle of financial confidence. Anything that makes you feel otherwise is always up for discussion.

I can't afford the minimums to open a brokerage account. Are there other options for me to purchase stock or mutual funds?
Yes. Go online and research discount brokerage firms or even mutual fund companies that are available to you. Many of them typically offer accounts that are geared to help new investors save on a recurring cycle. Many of them offer discounts on the minimum balance or waivers,

assuming you participate in a deposit program on a monthly, quarterly or annual basis. As it relates to stock, you can research a specific stock by going to its company website and clicking on the Investor Relations tab. It will identify who the company stock uses as their transfer agent. Contact the transfer agent to get any information regarding a DRIP (Direct Reinvestment Plan) Plan that can help you purchase specific stock shares with no transaction fees. This is just one of many alternative ways of building an investment portfolio with minimal costs and tracking your journey toward a lifestyle of wealth and wellness!

Taxes, Estate Planning & Insurance

What are the four basic strategies for minimizing total taxes?

The four basic tax strategies to help minimize total taxes are tax avoidance, tax reduction, tax deferral and income conversion. Hold on….Tax Avoidance is NOT what you may think it is. It is not simply running away from your tax responsibilities. **Tax Avoidance** is a strategy that produces an economic return that is not subject to taxation. The best example of this is a tax-exempt security. Interest received from securities so defined is exempt from federal taxation and in specific situations, exempt from state taxation as well. **Tax Reduction** involves deductions and credits that are used to reduce your taxable income. Some charitable gifting results in a reduction of the client's current overall tax obligation. Contributions made to certain forms of retirement accounts (IRAs, SEP-IRAs, Keogh Plans,

401k plans, etc.) have the effect of reducing that individual's total taxable income. Also, deductions for home mortgage interest, property taxes and state and local income taxes all reduce the taxable income, assuming the taxpayer has enough deductions to itemize deductions. That's why it's important to know the rules of the game, if you're going to play. It makes no sense for a person who makes a lot of income to NOT be a homeowner, you essential have the opportunity to build wealth through real estate, and at the same time reduce your taxable income. Renters don't have this option. **Tax Deferral** allows an investment to grow over time, allowing the growth in value to not be recognized for current tax purposes. Cash value life insurance is an example of a tax-deferred investment. Other investments are tax deferred when they are held inside an IRA, SEP-IRA, Keogh account, or tax-deferred annuity. Interest, dividends, and capital gains build up over time in these accounts, but they are only taxed at some point in the future when the client withdraws funds from the account. Income Conversion is a strategy that may be more versed for a high-income earner. The logic behind this strategy is to convert ordinary income to capital gains. Since higher-income clients generally pay a higher tax rate on ordinary income, they can benefit if they convert that income to long-term capital gains, which are taxed at a lower rate. Investing in growth stocks is one approach to income conversion.

Family / Estate Planning ....Leaving a Legacy!

Why is it important to have a will?

Without a will or any other estate planning document in place, when you die your assets will be disbursed following your state's laws for such situations. This is called dying intestate. It doesn't matter if you told a loved one or wrote it down on a piece of paper, if you don't have a will the state gets to decide how your assets are distributed.

What are some other ways to avoid probate if you don't have a will?

For retirement assets, making sure you have the proper beneficiaries in place, can help you to pass assets to family members or whoever you have listed as a recipient of assets in case anything were to happen to you. Outside of retirement accounts, you can establish registrations on taxable assets called TODs (Transfer on Death) that avoid probate as well. Lastly, one of the most efficient ways to avoid probate on assets is setting up a trust account. Trusts offer numerous ways of legal protection under the law especially for those with assets in excess of $100,000, where assets can avoid probate due to small estate laws. Even for homes and other property held outside of cash, you can either look into forming the legal entity of a trust as owner to extend the life and legacy of ownership without leaving it to your state to decide. Contact a legal advisor for your specific situation. For those who may be unable to afford an attorney, check with your employer to see if they offer pre-paid legal service packages that you can purchase and have an attorney produce the major legal documents that you should have in place.

Healthcare & Insurance

Why is medical & life insurance important in building a lifestyle of wealth & wellness? I really don't understand why many Americans have historically gone without insurance for the sake of saving a little money, or the best answer yet, "I can't afford it!" You actually can't afford to NOT have insurance. Of course with Obamacare, the Patient Protection and Affordable Care Act of 2010 instituted through the Obama Administration, you are now required to enforce medical insurance or risk being penalized for lack of coverage. Insurance planning is one of the most important line items to your maintaining a balanced, healthy and happy home. Did you know that medical bills are the #1 leading cause of bankruptcy in the United States? That's right, not credit card bills or a blatant abandonment of financial responsibilities. So making sure we have proper medical insurance coverage is key to prevention of major medical issues that could be extremely costly when unaddressed for extensive periods of time. The same can be said about life insurance coverage. Just like car insurance, you think to yourself why do we have to pay to have this coverage when you've never had an accident or any major traffic incident but when it happens you are surely glad that you had coverage in place. There is no amount of money that makes up for lack of life insurance coverage. Even wealthy individuals maintain proper life insurance coverage to make sure unforeseeable events don't stop them from properly taking care of their families and providing income replacement for goals and lifestyle accommodations to be maintained even in their absence. It is one of the many reasons why some of us continue cycles of poverty and start over with every generation because instead of leaving a legacy and financial responsibility behind, we inherit funeral expenses and an outstanding list of financial obligations in our time of grief. This should not ever have to be the case. Let's all play our part in leaving a legacy for our families and our community that can be sustained for generations!

What are the pros and cons of Group Life Insurance through work?

Some of the pros to buying insurance through your employer include: convenience, price and acceptance. Convenience is key to those who know they need life insurance but haven't bought it yet. Getting coverage through work can be the easiest way to protect your family. It can also be a good deal, sometimes offering rates you can't beat by shopping around. Finally, people with serious medical conditions may qualify for a much better rate through the group policy that they could not get on their own. A medical exam is not required, although you might have to fill out a detailed questionnaire. Some of the disadvantages of group life insurance include separating from an employer, costs and lack of sufficient coverage. When you separate from your employer, you may be able to convert your group policy into individual life insurance but it will be a whole life policy that is much more expensive than a term policy. Keep in mind if you have a serious medical condition, timing is everything. Some employers only give you a 30 or 60 day window to decide on keeping the policy in place without having to do a medical exam and your expenses could immediately go up to maintain coverage. Lastly, most employers limit the amount of coverage that is offered through them based upon your annual salary. Once you begin looking at larger amounts of coverage for income replacement, you may be better off seeking outside coverage with an insurance provider with term policies that offers greater flexibility and pricing.

What literature do most investment/financial service firms offer that address the needs of minority communities?

✓ I can tell you there are not many. The fact that firms like Ariel Funds in their annual minority investor survey shows that African-Americans lag behind other race groups as it relates to savings, workplace retirement plan participation, etc. shed some light as to where the problems exist.

✓ Education and livable wages are directly correlated to identifying groups that charge ahead versus those that fall behind. This is no secret since many sociologists including one of my favorites, Dr. Thomas Shapiro, has thoroughly researched the epidemic of a widening social inequality gap that is largely due to race and economics.

✓ Let's not diminish our teaching of miracles, signs and wonders…..but surely we need to ramp up our teaching of financial literacy and stewardship targeting the African-American church. Personally, I'm tired of seeing the saints of God struggle in their belief system due to the direct lack of sufficiency and poverty that permeates our world, our community and our church.

✓ Many investment firms don't offer accounts that are for entry level investors who only have enough to setup a recurring investment plan to build their nest egg. While, there are some who do, more than likely that entry-level investor is still struggling with daily and monthly commitments as it relates to household items that prevent them from investing on a consistent, long-term basis.

So while our brothers and sisters are consistently engaging in "miracle" seed giving, we have yet to offer Christian believers the opportunity to address their flaws, confront their habits, and implement a **Disciplined Action Plan** that will reduce debt, create more job opportunities, pursue advanced earning wages or learn fundamental investment strategies to building wealth!

***Disclosure: For your specific situation, please see an investment professional who can review your profile and make specific recommendations in accordance to that investment profile. The information contained in these responses does not constitute an offer of investment advice. Please see an Investment professional prior to making any decisions regarding your portfolio. ***

APPENDIX

Declarations & Activation for Financial Breakthrough, Prosperity & Overflow

———◆———

Father, in the name of Jesus, I thank you for being the God who has promised me that I will be glad and shout for joy, because I favor your righteous cause. You take PLEASURE in the PROSPERITY of your servant, according to Psalm 35:27.

Lord, I understand that if I seek you first and your righteousness, all things shall be added unto me. (Matth. 6:33) So I declare that as a covenant giver and sower of your kingdom that you will give unto me, GOOD MEASURE, PRESSED DOWN, SHAKEN TOGETHER, AND RUNNING OVER.

I am the Joseph, Nehemiah and Amos of my generation. I am a kingdom strategist and visionary for my family, my church and those who need financial breakthrough in their lives. I am the difference-maker that you have called from the pit to the palace. Favor is on my life. Prosperity is on my life. Overflow is on my life. Grace abounds toward me, that I may have all sufficiency in all things and to every good work.

Lord, as I submit my life to you as a covenant giver, bringing my tithes and all the firsts of my increase into your storehouse, you will give me a storehouse, a place where I can build and get wealth that will be sustained for generations to come. Open up the windows of heaven, pour out a blessing that is exceeding abundant above all that I can ask or think.

Lord I declare and decree that you have promised me that you would rebuke the devourer for my sake. Money cometh unto me! You have given me the P.O.W.E.R. to Get WEALTH! Provision, Opportunities, Wisdom, Experience and Resilience cometh unto me! I am a MONEY MAGNET! Lord I agree and partner with you today, that the thoughts and Provision you've placed in my mind, will bring great wealth into my hands. Lord I declare, that I am strategically aligned and a partner of the kingdom assignment you desire to fulfill in the earth. Today, I take my rightful position to GET IN THE GAME! Wealth, wisdom and riches are in my house! Every experience of my past, both good and bad, are NOW working together for my good! And because your POWER goes before me, I declare the counsel and wisdom of God that teaches my hands to war and my fingers to fight,

WAR UNTIL I WIN. Just like the army that went before King Jehosophat, my WAR of PRAYER, my WAR OF PRAISE, my WAR OF PURPOSE, will bring me a PERFORMANCE that my seed and generations beyond me will celebrate.

I declare and decree, new ideas, vision, and entrepreneurial endeavors that will supply and sustain the needs of my family for generations to come!

I rebuke the spirit of poverty, lack and not enough. You have promised that I shall eat the good of the land. I declare and decree that there is nothing lacking, nothing missing, and nothing broken. You are the God who shall supply all of my need according to your riches in glory! Because I am the Ambassador of Change for my family, I uproot all generational hindrances – situational and generational poverty – has no place in my family bloodline. Prosperity, overflow and abundance are for the GOOD OF MY HOUSE.

Yes indeed, it won't be long now. Things are going to happen so fast, my head will swim. One thing fast on the heels of the other; I won't be able to keep up. Everything will be happening at once – and everywhere I look, blessings! Blessings like wine pouring off the mountains and the hills. (Amos 9:13-15)

It is your will for me to prosper, and not be bound by the chains of debt. I acknowledge that everything in the heavens and the earth belong to you. I am a steward and you are the owner of all that I possess. Help me to be faithful with all of the resources you have placed under my care. Give me insight and wisdom in every area of finance – SOWING, SAVING, SPENDING, and SHARING. I pray for increase. Enlarge my territory so that I help others and further your kingdom in all that I do.

It is in the name of Jesus that I submit these requests for your earthly and kingdom assignments to be fulfilled in me, AMEN!

BIBLIOGRAPHY

Akbar, Na'im. Breaking the Chains of Psychological Slavery.
Tallahassee: Mind Productions, 1996.

Alcorn, Randy. Managing God's Money: A Biblical Guide.
Carol Stream: Tyndale House Publishers, 2011.

Brookfield, Stephen D. and Stephen Preskill. Learning As a Way of
Leading: Lessons from the Struggle for Social Justice.
San Francisco: Jossey-Bass, 2009.

Bonhoeffer, Dietrich. The Cost of Discipleship.
New York: Touchstone, 1995.

Burrell, Tom. Brainwashed: Challenging the Myth of Black nferiority.
New York: SmileyBooks, 2010.

DuBois, W.E.B. The Talented Tenth.
Lexington: 2014.

Isaac, Patrick. Societal Reform: Taking the Kingdom to the Systems.
Quebec: Dunamis Productions, 2014.

Jenkins, Lee. Lee Jenkins on Money: Real Solutions to
Financial Challenges.
Chicago: Moody Publishers, 2009.

Myers, Bryant. Walking with the Poor: Principles and Practices of
Transformational Development.
Maryknoll: Orbis Books, 2011.

Murdock, Mike. Seven Laws You Must Honor to Have
Uncommon Success.
Wisdom International, 2011.

Rauschenbusch, Walter. A Theology for the Social Gospel.
Louisville: Westminster John Knox Press, 1997.

Shapiro, Thomas M. The Hidden Cost of Being African American:
How Wealth Perpetuates Inequality.
New York: Oxford University Press, 2004.

Thompson, Dr. Leroy. Money Cometh: To the Body of Christ.
Tulsa: Harrison House, 1999.

Warnock, Raphael. The Divided Mind of the Black Church:
Theology, Piety and Public Witness.
New York: New York University Press, 2014.

West, Cornel. Race Matters.

    New York: Vintage Books, 2001.

Spors, Kelly. "Traditional IRA vs. Roth IRA." www.rothira.com, Investopedia, LLC, 2018

"The Basics on Catch-Up Contributions in 401k Plans." http://www.401khelpcenter.com/catch-up_contributions.html#.W0D2qNJKjlV. 401khelpcenter.com, LLC, 2018

"Pros and Cons of Group Life Insurance Through Work." https://www.nerdwallet.com, NerdWallet, Inc. 17-5-17

"Poverty in Black America." www.blackdemographics.com, US Bureau of the Census, 2014

"Ariel Investments 2015 Black Investor Survey." https://www.arielinvestments.com. Ariel Investments, LLC. 2-2-16

"Prosperity Theology"

    https://en.wikipedia.org/wiki/Prosperity_theology

"The Joseph Principle in Action" Notes from www.cfaith.com

"Studies Regarding Poverty" on www.worldvisionusprograms.org, retrieved on Jan. 13th, 2018

Motley Fool's Most Pervasive Myths About Rich People on www.fool.com/retirement/2017/04/06/7 retrieved January 2018000000